CONNOLLYS IN THE KITCHEN

Then and Now: 2016

Mynchen's Field Press
46 Raheny Park
Raheny, Dublin 5, Ireland
www.mynchensfieldpress.com

Published by:
Mynchen's Field Press
46 Raheny Park, Raheny
Dublin 5,
Ireland

ISBN: 978-1530891306
ISBN: 1530891302

DEDICATED

To the departed generations of Connollys, Murphys, Dunleas, Kanes, extended families and friends to whom we owe our love of the special recipes presented in this book.

TABLE OF CONTENTS

INTRODUCTION

There was a time when any discussion on cookbooks centered on <u>The Betty Crocker Cookbook</u>, <u>Joy of Cooking</u> or the <u>Better Homes and Gardens Cookbook</u> (ring-binder). Families had one or more of these staples and that was about it. Today there are thousands of cookbooks with hundreds more introduced every year, particularly at Christmas. The explosion in the number of celebrity chefs (thank you Julia Child) documenting and publishing their revelations to the culinary world, contributes significantly to the abundance of cookbooks found in family kitchens. At last count, Robert and Pamela admit to having in excess of fifty cookbooks, few of which are ever opened.

So why, one might reasonably inquire, should the Connolly Family be publishing a cookbook? Quite simple, we believe that about 99% of cooking has nothing to do with mass-published cookbooks. In day-to-day meal planning, and even on special occasions, nearly everyone reverts to time-honored, tried and true family recipes. We all have memories of those special dishes prepared by mothers, fathers, aunts, uncles or grandparents and want to share some of those eating experiences with our children. Our "go-to recipes" are the ones we have prepared many times and are confident will be a special treat whenever they are served. Consequently, if we are having family or friends over for dinner or a cookout, it would be a very brave person who would go hunting for recipes in a celebrity cookbook. Of course, we experiment, even with traditional recipes, because that is what good cooks do. In the end, we revert to what we know and love.

This, *Connollys in the Kitchen,* contains our own favorites, concocted and perfected over several generations. Even now, the younger family members are adding to this collection presenting new treats or adjusting the old recipes with different or perhaps healthier – perish the thought – options. Maybe in twenty or thirty years there will be a second edition, but for now, we present our favorites.

Quite apart from being a collection of recipes, this book records memories of those special days and nights when we celebrated together with something to eat…or drink. We have included stories and pictures to provide a bit of family context and history, something no celebrity cookbook could dream of providing. Hopefully, we have also provided some insight into the special people, related or not, who touched our lives and contributed to making our family what it is. You will undoubtedly notice that this book is written in the first person plural. That is because no one has individually written this collection rather we have all contributed and it is the story of our combined culinary experiences. It is important, however, that we say a bit more about this "royal we" which includes well over one hundred years of the extended Connolly family. For convenience purposes only, we are using Pat, Robert, John, Michael, Mary, Sheila, Anne and Joan as the 'base generation.' When this book mentions 'Mom' or 'Dad,' the reference is to the base generation's parents. Of course, this is not where our story begins, or ends.

Although Pat and Anne would be the experts on such things and can provide far greater detail on the family genealogy and history, we will start with a brief synopsis. John Joseph Murphy, was an employee of Swift and Company at the Union Stockyards in Chicago. He married Hanora Emily "Birdie"

Dunlea – 'Gram or Grammy' who emigrated from Cork in 1901. She worked as toll operator for the Illinois Bell Telephone Company. They had four children, John Joseph (who died as an infant), Eileen Mary Agnes, John Michael and Francis Joseph. Eileen 'Mom' is the matriarch of the base generation and for most of her younger years lived in Brookfield, Illinois.

Moving to the Connolly side, Robert Emmet Connolly was Vice President of Finance for the Illinois Central Railroad (whose headquarters was in New York because most of the directors thought Chicago was a hick-town) and married Mary Theresa Kane 'Nanna' in New York. They had four children, Robert Emmet, (who died in infancy) Mary Theresa, Richard Joseph and Catharine Mary (Cath). In 1938, the Illinois Central Railroad opened an office in Chicago and the Connollys moved to Flossmoor, Illinois. Their house on Bunker Road remained in the family until Cath, nearly 92 years of age, died in 2012. Richard Joseph 'Dad' is the patriarch of the base generation.

After spending three years during World War II manning an advance radar post in New Guinea, Dad returned to Chicago taking a job with the Federal Milk Market administration. Fortunately, Mom was already employed in their Chicago office. There are two versions relating to the couple's first encounter. According to Mom, she spotted Dad soon after he was employed and remarked, "Where did Erdmann get the Irishman?" According to Lucile Wilhelm, Mom's best friend and eventual maid of honor, Mom was heard to remark, "There is my Irishman!" a story which Mom steadfastly denied. It is of little consequence because there were obviously sparks going both ways which brings to mind the old adage, "Boy chases girl until she catches him." Richard and Eileen were married on December 27, 1947. They had nine children: Patricia Mary, Kathleen Mary (died at age five) Robert Emmet, John Joseph, Michael Paul, Mary Theresa, Sheila Mary, Anne Maureen and Joan Mary. The first two were born in Chicago Heights, the next four in Milwaukee and the last three in Fort Wayne where the 'base generation' spent most of its formative years, living at 4305 McMillen Park Drive. Ultimately, Mom moved to a villaminium on Ridge Valley Drive where she spent her later years.

Our current snapshot in time shows that Pat, a teacher, married Jack Ready, a lawyer and settled in Monroe, Michigan. They have four children, James (who died at birth), Joseph, Daniel and Máire who married Ben DeLand. Robert, a lawyer, married Pamela Burke, a teacher, and settled in Raheny, Dublin, Ireland. John, a hardware store owner, married Julie Van Horn, a nutritionist, and settled in Fort Wayne, Indiana. They have three children, Christopher, Kasey and Eian. Michael a hardware store owner, married Ewelina Podzielinski, a mental health counselor, and settled in Fort Wayne, Indiana. Michael has four children. Richard, who married Molly Evans and has a daughter-Caroline; Lauren, who married Mitch Mathews and has a child on the way...or as Lauren reports, in keeping with our cooking theme, "in the oven," Katy, and Eli (born to Michael and Ewelina). Michael also has two step-children, John and Sarah Podzielinski. Mary, a sales manager, married Mike McManus, a podiatrist and settled in Fort Wayne, Indiana. They have three children, Billy, who is engaged to Katie Leeuw, Sean and Emily. Sheila, an events coordinator, settled in Cincinnati, Ohio but spends most of her time visiting or hosting family members. Anne, a pediatric neurologist settled in St. Louis, Missouri. She has four children, Caitlin, who is engaged to Nick Safley, Colin, Conor and Cormac. Joan, a sales executive, married Kevin, an account executive, and settled in South Bend, Indiana. They have four children, James, Luke, Patrick and Liam.

Nearly everyone in this snapshot participated in this project by providing favorite recipes, stories or pictures so they are all part of the "royal we." As a result, we fully expect that each copy of this book will, in no time at all, become dog-eared and stained, well-loved and well-worn and that is as it should be.

BREAKFAST AND BRUNCH

Breakfast at 4305 McMillen Park Drive was, according to Mom, the most important meal of the day. As a result, before we were packed off to school...verrrry early in the morning, we ate breakfast. On school days during the cold winter months that meant either hot oatmeal, also known as porridge, hot farina which was similar to oatmeal but a bit smoother, or cocoa wheats – a special treat. Some of us were not fans of any of those choices but, provided enough, milk, brown sugar and/or raisins smothered the mush, it was tolerable. When the weather was warmer, on Saturdays, or during the summer, a wide selection of cereals was available with an ample supply of frozen orange juice. Sunday morning, however, was the opportunity for a more interesting breakfast, especially on special occasions like Easter when kidney stew was served. Sunday began with the drive to St. Henry's and Mass at, if memory serves, 8:30 or 9:00 a.m. We were all dressed in our Sunday best, including suits and ties for the boys and dresses, hats and gloves for the girls. We would take our place on the right side of the church, viewed looking at the altar, because those pews were longer than the middle sections. Other larger families also sat on our side of the church particularly the Hipskinds who were usually a pew or two ahead of us. Mom occasionally commented that all the other boys in the parish seemed to tower over their fathers, but not so with the Connollys who apparently inherited shorter genes. As Mom's second cousin. Joe Walsh in Howth, Ireland, was fond of remarking, "It is a great thing to be a fine tall man, but how many fine tall old men do you see walking around? Anyway, back to the breakfast. We all learned to feed ourselves using Royal Doulton Bunnykins bowls which Gram bought for us at Marshall Field's in Chicago. Each bowl had an illustration of a bunny scene and an overhanging lip which made scooping food a bit easier. At about the same time as Gram was purchasing a Bunnykins bowl for Joan, Pamela's Grand Aunt Marie was buying one for Pamela at Switzer's in Dublin. Remarkably, some 44 years later, Robert compared his bowl with Pamela's and the result can be seen on the previous page. Clearly a match made in heaven. More standard Sunday fare included bacon and eggs, or cans of canned corned beef hash, pancakes or an occasional waffle. In recent times, brunch has become popular and is included in this section as well.

Luke - never too early to cook breakfast

Corned Beef Hash

On occasion, Dad would corn a lump of beef in an earthenware crock which was kept under the basement stairs. This process would entail soaking the beef in a brine over several weeks with the resulting dinner becoming an exceptional feast. In later years, corned beef was regularly available in the grocery store so corned beef, cabbage and boiled potatoes were an occasional Saturday dinner and always served on St. Patrick's Day. A Sunday breakfast of corned beef hash took care of the abundant leftovers. Mom used the food grinding attachment to her Mixmaster to simplify the process. This recipe anticipates no such gadget.

The Ingredients:
- *cooked corned beef, potatoes, onions*

The Recipe:
- *Chop cooked brisket of corned beef into small bits.*
- *Chop an equal amount of peeled and boiled potatoes into similar small bits.*
- *Dice a couple of medium sized onions…significantly less volume than the corned beef/potatoes.*
- *Mix the ingredients thoroughly and fry with butter and a bit of oil (stops the butter from burning).*
- *Serve with plenty of Worcestershire sauce.*

Adjustments:
Rather than using peeled Idaho or similar white potatoes, red-skinned new potatoes or any soft-skinned potato boiled and chopped with the skin on, provides an interesting change, particularly as

13

the skin will crisp differently than the meat and centers of the potatoes. A number of people find that a poached egg provides just the right finish. Rye bread was the choice as an accompaniment but, of course, English muffins, especially left over from the pizza, are a great alternative.

Robert and Cormac – corned beef hashing

Brunch Casserole

This recipe is courtesy of Cele Wilhelm who was Mom's maid of honor and best friend growing up in Brookfield. Mary discovered it among Mom's collection and sent it on. Cele, whose mother, like Gram, came from Ireland was as Irish as they came, despite the frustrating fact that her mother married a German fellow. Cele, a registered nurse and Robert's god-mother, never missed remembering him on his birthday or at Christmas.   After retiring, Cele and her friend Marion, accompanied Fr. Neenan (more on him later) on his many travels and the trio became frequent visitors at Ridge Valley. Shortly after the Royal Couple married, (Robert and Pamela are frequently referred to as the Royal Couple as they are treated as royalty whenever they return to the United States - or were so treated when Cath was alive.) Cele, at age 85 made a special trip to Dublin for a most memorable visit. Although this recipe was not frequently enjoyed, it does provide for a proper and filling brunch.

The Ingredients:
- *white bread, American/cheddar cheese, eggs, milk, salt, pepper, bacon*

The Recipe:
- *Spread 12 slices of buttered and cubed white bread in a 9x13 buttered baking pan.*
- *Layer ½ lb. American or cheddar cheese-cubed and the bread.*
- *Scramble 6 eggs, add a splash of milk and dash of salt.*
- *Pour mixture over the bread/cheese ensuring the bread absorbs the eggs.*
- *Cover with foil and refrigerate overnight.*
- *Bake at 300° for 1½ hours.*
- *Shortly before removing from oven sprinkle 8 slices cooked crispy and crumbled bacon over the casserole.*
- *Cut into squares and serve immediately.*

Adjustments:
Cele suggests that chicken or ham can be added by cubing the meat and adding it as an additional

15

layer with the cheese cubes. This recipe serves 6-8 persons so it can be reduced proportionately for fewer people.

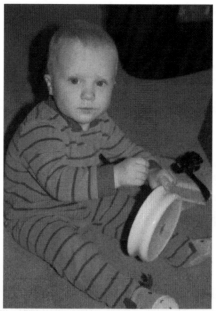

Eli - Who else has my Bunnykins bowl?

Breakfast Frittata

As we would all know from visits to Sheila and Linda at various holiday destinations, we can count on a wonderful breakfast frittata to start the day off right. The only downside is that their frittatas are entirely too healthy with plenty of veggies. Of course, toast or English muffins with plenty of butter and preserves will help in that regard. This recipe comes from Linda Maier, Luke's godmother and our 'sista from a different mista,' and Sheila claims it tastes best in Hilton Head or on Given Road in Cincinnati.

16

The Ingredients:

- *eggs, garlic, olive oil, mushrooms, asparagus, broccoli, Parmesan cheese, salt, pepper, cayenne pepper flakes (or Tabasco)*

The Recipe:

- *Sauté in a large, oven safe skillet, ½ large diced onion and 2 minced garlic cloves in 2 tbsp. olive oil.*
- *Add, while continuing to sauté, 1 cup sliced mushrooms, 1 cup finely chopped asparagus, 1 cup finely chopped broccoli.*
- *In a separate bowl, beat 6 eggs and add ½ cup milk, dash of salt, dash of pepper, dash of cayenne pepper flakes (or Tabasco) to taste.*
- *Pour egg mixture into the frying pan covering the sautéed vegetables and top with a layer of shredded Parmesan cheese.*
- *Place skillet in oven pre-heated to 375° F. for 18 to 20 minutes checking after 12 minutes as cooking time may vary depending on the oven and the skillet.*
- *Remove and slice into pie size pieces and serve hot.*

Adjustments:

Some people prefer egg beaters and egg whites to proper eggs and that is certainly permitted. Use enough eggbeaters/whites (eliminating the milk) to completely cover the sautéed vegetables. There is no problem making a large frittata as leftovers can be covered and refrigerated and then reheated in a microwave for 24 seconds.

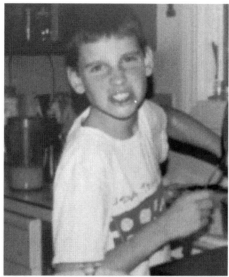

James - and I have to do the dishes as well

Sweet Crepes

This recipe was presented by Joe when he was a wee slip of a lad. As he now finds himself quite comfortable experimenting and trying out new recipes, perhaps this was a sign of things to come.

The Ingredients:
- *all-purpose flour, salt, eggs, milk, butter, lemon, juice, sugar*

The Recipe:
- *Sift ½ cup all-purpose flour and a pinch of salt into a mixing bowl.*

- *Crack 2 eggs into the center of the flour and whisk the egg and flour together.*
- *Mix 1 cup milk, 1/3 cup water and slowly pour into flour/egg whisking the mixture until smooth.*
- *Melt a thick slice of butter into a skillet to cover the bottom of the pan.*
- *Pour a thin layer of batter into the pan and cook until the bottom of the crepe is golden.*
- *Turn the crepe and top with lemon juice and sugar.*
- *Serve hot off the griddle.*

Lamb Kidney Stew

Kidney Stew was a delicacy reserved for very special occasions, such as after Mass on Easter morning. Although not popular with everyone in the family, those of us who enjoyed this treat hoped the others' tastes would not "mature." Kidney stew is a distinctively Irish dish that came into the family from Nanna who brought it from New York to Chicago. While the big cities had a strong Irish-American population, Fort Wayne did not. Acquiring lamb, whether it be chops, legs or kidneys was not as simple as heading to the local grocery store. There was a butcher named Heiny who saved various cuts of lamb for Mom. She collected his offerings when they were available, put them into plastic bags and stored them in the freezer. When enough was accumulated, we had broiled chops or kidney stew. Unfortunately, Mom created her stew version from memory and a written record has not been discovered. When Pamela travelled to the Fort the Easter before the Royal Couple married, there was great consternation about the sauce. She volunteered that it sounded like a roux to her, so she was promptly put in charge. What she didn't understand was that cooking for 15-20 is a major undertaking while a roux, which

19

requires continuous stirring, is typically made in small measures. Pamela claims that she could hardly lift her arm for days.

The Ingredients:
- *lamb kidneys, butter, flour, milk, salt, pepper, canned mushrooms*

The Recipe:
- *Clean 10-12 lamb kidneys. (This entails pulling/cutting off every vein, stringy bit, fatty bit and discoloration… a long and arduous process) and cutting them into bite-sized pieces.*
- *Cook kidney bits in boiling water until they are tender but firm.*
- *In a double boiler at low heat melt 4 tbsp. butter.*
- *Blend in slowly, 4 tbs. flour, ½ tsp. salt, ¼ tsp. pepper.*
- *Increase heat and add 2 cups milk, stirring constantly until the sauce nearly boils, then reduce heat.*
- *Drain kidneys through a sieve keeping the bits that might have dislodged during boiling process and add to roux sauce.*
- *Add 1-2 cans of sliced mushrooms, to taste.*
- *Continue to heat, stirring frequently so the sauce does not stick to the sides and the stew reaches a thick and rich consistency.*
- *Serve on plates with English muffins - to soak up the excess sauce.*

Adjustments:
The proportions listed in this recipe can be easily adjusted to accommodate more or fewer kidneys

20

and/or diners. It would be permissible to use finely chopped, fresh mushrooms sautéed in butter as opposed to the canned variety. One major adjustment, undoubtedly a different recipe all together, is included here because we don't have a recipe for it either. Precious few of us enjoyed this treat. (Some believed that chewing tripe was akin to chewing a wet blanket.) Quite simply, instead of kidneys, cut honeycomb tripe (the lining of a cow's stomach) into small squares, boil until it is tender, eliminate the mushrooms, add it to the roux sauce and serve.

Mary, Mom, Anne, Joan, Sheila, Pat - ♪ I'll wear my Easter bonnet

Salt Mackerel

Salt mackerel is another delicious east coast dish which rarely appeared but was greatly appreciated by nearly everyone. Because Fort Wayne is a long way from the ocean and mackerel is an ocean fish, it's availability in the Midwest was limited at best. Remarkably Mom occasionally was able to purchase the fish. In travelling to Ireland many of us discovered that cooking fish in this manner for breakfast was quite normal as kippers (typically herring) was served at many hotels. The recipe is quite simple, although the preparation time is significantly longer because mackerel is extremely salty, some of which is best removed. Mom had an oblong aluminum pot that she used for just this purpose.

The Ingredients:
- *mackerel filets, butter, pepper*

The Recipe:
- *Soak mackerel filets (headless, tailless, boned and halved with the skin on) in fresh water for at least a couple of days changing the water at least twice a day.*
- *Broil skin side up until the skins brown slightly.*
- *Turn filets, skin side down, slather with butter and broil until brown with crispy edges.*
- *Pepper to taste and enjoy with toast and plenty of water.*

Caramelized Onion, Mushroom, and Goat Cheese Quiche

Cait presents her brunch specialty, a wonderful quiche, which obviously, requires a great deal of preparation. We are impressed with the next generation's interest in offering recipes which require considerable time and attention to detail. This is a perfect example...except for the store bought pie crust. Considering the quality of these crusts, and the fact that they weren't available years ago, we will give Cait, and anyone who uses them, our blessing.

The Ingredients:
- 9" pie crust, olive oil, butter, cremini mushrooms, onions, marsala wine, salt, pepper, goat cheese, dill, eggs, half and half, ground yellow mustard

The Recipe:
- Refrigerate home-made or purchased 9" pie crust.
- Sauté in large frying pan over medium to low heat, 5 oz. sliced cremini mushrooms and 1 diced small yellow onion, in 1 tbsp. butter and 1 tbsp. olive oil until onions are golden and mushrooms have a nice sear (about 15 minutes.)
- Increase heat to medium-high and add 1-2 tbsp. Marsala wine. Stir until wine evaporates.
- Season mushroom/onion mixture with salt and pepper and set aside.
- In a medium sized mixing bowl, scramble 4 eggs then add ¾ cup half and half, ½ tsp. salt, ¼ tsp. black pepper, ½ tsp. ground yellow mustard.
- Remove pie crust from refrigerator and scatter onion/mushroom mixture evenly over the base.
- Sprinkle 3 oz. crumbled goat cheese and 1 tsp. chopped basil over the onion/mushroom layer.
- Pour egg mixture over previous layers.
- Bake in a preheated oven at 375° for 40-45 minutes until golden brown and cooked through.
- Allow to cool for 10 minutes before serving.

Connollys in the Kitchen: Then and Now, 2016

LUNCH AND SOUPS

 When we were old enough, we were pretty much on our own to prepare and eat whatever we preferred for lunch.   On Sundays during the school year, everyone made a week's supply of sandwiches (Some individuals requiring two or three for each day.). Names were written on each bagged sandwich along with a note if lettuce was to be added. They were then put in the freezer. Every morning Mom would write names on paper bags, line them up, distribute the sandwiches - including lettuce if so noted - and add other lunch items such as cookies, fruit or chips. Sandwiches were then, and continue to be, a favorite lunch item. We know that a couple of us enjoy peanut butter and lettuce sandwiches even to this day.   Other popular sandwich choices included peanut butter and jelly, jelly and cream cheese on rye, leftover meat when available, (This would certainly include meat loaf with a bit of ketchup, lettuce and Swiss cheese.), bologna, ham with mustard, lunch meats and a number of variations. The common denominator was plenty of butter...even on peanut butter sandwiches. As we grew older, on weekends or when school was out, some of us exercised our culinary skills grilling hamburgers, fish stick sandwiches, grilled cheese, leftovers

25

(e.g. spaghetti), macaroni and cheese, hot dogs or soups (typically Campbell's from a can). The following lunch recipes include more gourmet delights. The recipes are not all "ours" from the old/new days, but include contributions from many sources.

Reuben Sandwich

The Reuben was a particular favorite. Mom had an electric grill which could accommodate about six sandwiches at one time. Left-over corned beef was the best but delicatessen corned beef was also occasionally available. Of course, Jewish rye from the bakery in Brookfield was the very best.

The Ingredients:
- *rye bread, butter, Swiss cheese, corned beef, horseradish, sauerkraut*

The Recipe:
- *Butter outsides of rye bread and place butter side down on the frying pan/grill.*
- *Add slice of Swiss cheese topped with corned beef.*
- *Top with second slice of rye bread, butter side out.*
- *Grill until bread is toasted and turn to toast the other side.*
- *Serve hot with a pickle/chips.*

Adjustments
The primary adjustment to this culinary delight involved ingredients. Many of us added volumes of horseradish sauce (creamed was allowed) on top of the corned beef, according to taste. Some

of us also added canned sauerkraut on top of the beef or, even another slice of Swiss cheese, which meant cheese was oozing out of both sides.

Colin - someday I will throw a hammer

Chili

Occasionally, a big pot of chili was prepared to take the chill off a winter Saturday. Mom experimented with many recipes and other recipes were developed over the years. We have included two recipes in this section. The first comes from Joe Kernan, a good friend of the O'Connor Family who apart from being a Viet Nam war hero, was also the Mayor of South Bend and the Governor of Indiana. Joe would serve it before Notre Dame football games and Joan passes along the recipe. The second is a more generic, but very similar recipe, prepared by Mom for lunch and occasional Saturday dinner consumption.

Joe Kernan's Chili

The Ingredients:
- ground beef, kidney beans, green peppers, onions tomatoes, tomato paste, salt, black pepper, sugar, cheddar cheese, sour cream

The Recipe:
- Mix in large pot (or crock pot); 3 lbs. browned ground beef/chuck/round, 2 3 oz. cans of red kidney beans-crushed, 1 cup chopped green peppers, 3 cups chopped onions, 2 28 oz. cans of tomatoes, 2 12 oz. cans of tomato paste, 4 cups water, 1 tbsp. black pepper, 1 tbsp. salt, ¼ cup sugar.
- Simmer at low temperature for an hour or more, stirring often, or cook in crock pot for several hours so the flavors blend.
- Serve in a bowl, piping hot.

Adjustments:
Joe claims the key to this recipe is crushing the kidney beans, but slow cooking, particularly with a crock pot also contributes. Some people like to stir in a good handful of shredded cheddar cheese which melts into the chili and/or a dollop of sour cream to add a cool taste. Others like to add crumbled soda crackers or oyster crackers for a bit more texture.

Mom's Chili

The Ingredients:
- *ground beef, kidney beans, green peppers, onions, canned tomatoes, tomato paste, salt, chili powder, black pepper*

The Recipe:
- *Brown 2 lbs. ground beef in a skillet with 1 medium sized yellow onion.*
- *Transfer to large pot and add 2 diced green peppers, 1 tbsp. chili powder, 1 can red kidney beans – drained, one large can of tomatoes, 1 small can of tomato paste, ½ tsp. salt, ¼ tsp. pepper.*
- *Cook covered on low temperature for an hour or more until beans and peppers are soft.*
- *Serve in a bowl, piping hot with saltine crackers.*

Adjustments:
As with Joe's chili a good handful of cheddar cheese, which melts into the hot chili is an excellent touch.

Texas White Chili

While this recipe was originally discovered in the Detroit Free Press, over the many years since, Pat has perfected white chili. Traditionally, white chicken chili is served before the big Thanksgiving Turkey Bowl to fortify participants against the cold. While there are other adjustments available, when Pat dons her chef cap as a purist, she will cook down a stewing hen using both the broth and the chicken for this recipe. However, for this selection we will leave Pat to be the purist.

The Ingredients:
- white beans, olive oil, onion, garlic, green chilies, cumin, oregano, cinnamon, cayenne pepper, chicken, Monterey Jack cheese, sour cream, cilantro, green onions oyster crackers

The Recipe:
- Soak overnight 1 lb. small white beans. Drain and set aside just before cooking.
- Heat in a large soup pot 3 tbsp. olive oil and sauté one large minced onion, ends removed, until soft and translucent.
- Stir in 3 garlic cloves-peeled and minced, 8 oz. can of chopped green chilies, 1 tbsp. ground cumin, 1 tbsp. dried oregano, 1 tsp. ground cinnamon, pinch of cayenne pepper and sauté for 3 minutes.
- Add drained white beans and 8-10 cups of chicken broth.
- Bring to boil then reduce heat and simmer for 2-3 hours until beans are tender. If too dry, add additional broth.
- Stir in 4 cups of chopped chicken, salt and pepper to taste.
- Garnish with choice of: Monterey Jack cheese, salsa, sour cream, cilantro and/or green onions.
- Serve with oyster crackers or saltines.

Adjustments:
This recipe is an ideal opportunity to use leftover turkey or chicken and can be frozen for future

lunches on cold days. The proportions can be adjusted to account for the size of the crowed expected. Of course, it is always better to cook too much...and freeze the extras. A word from the expert....Pat is "heavy handed" on seasoning proportions.

John, Michael, Robert - way too much Christmas cheer

Turkey Chili

Completing a 'hat trick' of chilies we have Billy's specialty, Turkey Chili. It is ideal for those late autumn or winter afternoons and is guaranteed to take the 'chill' off you. Billy presents his recipe using ground turkey, meaning it can be created at any time. However, he has confirmed that replacing ground turkey with chopped leftovers would also be acceptable. So, if there was ever an answer to the age old question, "What do we do with leftover turkey at Thanksgiving or Christmas?" look no further.

The Ingredients:

- *ground turkey, olive oil, basil, onion powder, cumin, chili powder, garlic powder, flour, brown sugar, onion, garlic, green bell pepper, tomato sauce, canned diced tomatoes, great northern beans, black beans, canned corn, cornbread, goldfish crackers*

The Recipe:

- *Brown 1 pkg. (approximately 1¼ lb.) ground turkey in large skillet with 2 tbsp. olive oil.*
- *In a second pan, sauté ½ large white diced onion and 4 thinly sliced cloves of garlic in 1 tbsp. olive oil.*
- *After a few minutes cooking, add ½ chopped green bell pepper to the onion/garlic and cook until onion becomes transparent.*
- *Combine the browned turkey and vegetables in a large crock pot.*
- *Add to the crock pot 1 large can tomato sauce (app. 16 oz.), 1 12 oz. can of diced tomatoes (well-drained), 1 12 oz. can of corn (well-drained) 1 12 oz. can of great northern beans (well-drained), 1 12 oz. can of black beans, (well-drained) and thoroughly mix ingredients.*
- *Add tomato sauce from an additional 12 oz. can until desired thickness is achieved.*

- *Combine in a small bowl: 1 tsp. basil, 1 tbsp. onion powder, 2 tsp. cumin, 4 tsp. chili powder, 1 tbsp. cayenne pepper, 1 tbsp. garlic powder, 2 tbsp. all-purpose flour, 2 tbsp. brown sugar.*
- *While stirring the turkey/vegetable crock pot mixture, add the spice mix so it is evenly incorporated.*
- *Turning the crock pot on high, cook for 1½ to 2 hours stirring occasionally. Then turn heat down to low/warm and cook until it is time to serve (up to 12 hours).*
- *Serve with cornbread or goldfish crackers, if desired.*

Adjustments:

Billy suggests that if one prefers chili with a bit less 'heat,' use a smaller dose of chili powder and cayenne pepper in the spice mix. If using leftovers, turkey should be torn/pulled into smaller pieces and, as it is already cooked, will not require a great deal of pre-cooking.

Golden Gate Soup

This soup is nearly a meal in itself. Anne recommends this recipe which she acquired, in the style of her mother, from a magazine. The adjustments, adding different ingredients, turn the soup into Golden Gate Minestrone.

The Ingredients:

- *olive oil, onions, green pepper, carrots, white potatoes, celery, garlic, cans of tomatoes, V-8 juice, vegetable cubes, bay leaf, rosemary, parsley, zucchini, pasta, Parmesan cheese, yogurt*

The Recipe:

- *Mix 1/3 cup olive oil, 2 medium chopped onions, ½ chopped green pepper, 2 sliced medium carrots 2 medium white potatoes-sliced, 2 sliced stalks of celery, 2 minced cloves of garlic, 28 oz. can of tomatoes, 4 6 oz. cans of V-8 juice, 4 vegetable cubes, 1 bay leaf, 1 tsp. rosemary, 1 tsp. parsley, 2 small zucchini sliced, 2 cups pasta.*
- *Cook all ingredients on stove top or in crock pot.*
- *Garnish with Parmesan cheese or yogurt.*

Adjustments:

As is clear from this recipe, a wide variety of vegetables are included which provides scope for creative thinking, adding or eliminating as available. To create a minestrone add 1½ cups kidney beans (15½ oz. can), 1½ cups garbanzos (15½ oz. can) and 2 small yellow squash sliced in rounds.

Julie, Sheila, John - a bit of barbecue

Beef Barbecue

Lest any think that barbecue beef is a recent concoction, Pat presents Gram's recipe which has been passed down in her own distinct handwriting. Because Gram is not available to interpret, we have taken some minor liberties in the transcription. For example, the recipe calls for three pounds of lean beef and two pounds of pork, which might be a very interesting combination but, one suspects, that five pounds of either beef or pork can be used. On the other hand, Brendan Goggin, our third cousin from Cork (more on him later) sent us a stew recipe from 1918 that includes both beef and sausage so perhaps the two were used together. A combination of the different meats might make for an interesting experiment.

The Ingredients:
- *beef/pork onions, catsup, green pepper, white or brown sugar, cinnamon, cloves, vinegar, celery, lemon juice, Worcestershire sauce*

The Recipe:
- *In a skillet, brown 3 lbs. lean chopped beef (or 2 lbs. chopped pork) with a medium diced onion.*
- *Transfer browned meat to a cooking pot.*
- *Add 1 finely cut green pepper, 1 12 oz. bottle of catsup, 1 tbsp. white or brown sugar, 1 tsp. cinnamon, 1 tsp. crushed cloves, 2 tsp. vinegar, ½ cup finely chopped celery, 2 tsp. lemon juice, 1 tsp. Worcestershire sauce.*
- *Cook on a medium flame for about 15 minutes until the vegetables are soft.*
- *Serve hot on a bun.*

35

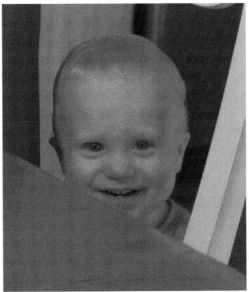

Eli - Where's my lunch?

Clam Chowder

Clam chowder has always been a favorite in the Connolly clan but typically originated in a Campbell's Soup can. Fortunately, Clam Chowder has been elevated to the heights with the contribution of Harumi Sasahara's version, served to hungry, cold football players after the Turkey Bowl. After moving to Monroe from Hiroshima, meeting at Joseph and Noriko's pre-school and becoming friends, the Sasaharas have joined us for the Thanksgiving extravaganza. Not only did clam chowder become an immensely delicious, popular and much appreciated event staple but valuable additions were made to the football game - Yuji, Noriko ('Nikki' and now also Ed), Kazuya (Kaz) and eventually, Kyoko. Lauren acquired this recipe and passes it on for our collection. As a Thanksgiving aside...Harumi and Pat

36

have had many fun, if not always successful years, bowling together - most recently as "Turkey Thyme!"

The Ingredients:
- *bacon, potatoes, onion, garlic powder, clam juice, canned clams, white wine, milk, heavy whipping cream, butter, fresh thyme, parsley, oyster crackers*

The Recipe:
- *Pan fry 6 slices of bacon, crumble and put aside.*
- *Peel and chop into small cubes 4 small to medium sized potatoes.*
- *Dice 1 large onion.*
- *Cook potatoes and onions in bacon grease.*
- *In large soup pot, mix 1½ tbsp. garlic powder, 1 cup clam juice (from drained clams), ½ cup white wine, 1 cup 2% milk, 1 cup heavy whip cream, 1 tbsp. butter, lots of fresh thyme. (Harumi is very generous with the thyme.)*
- *Add potatoes and onions and cook at medium heat.*
- *Crumble bacon and add 3-4 6½ oz. cans of drained clams to mix.*
- *Stir frequently and serve hot.*
- *Garnish with parsley and serve with oyster crackers or saltines.*

Julie, Kasey - another gourmet meal served

Spiced Lentil Soup with Coconut Milk

Julie presents this recipe as one of her favorites, a veritable Indian-Asian fusion dish. The fact that it originates with Julie should come as no surprise because, while Connolly recipes might reflect a "meat and potatoes" tradition, Julie adds a massive dose of interesting and different ingredients. These recipes are, perhaps, a bit more labor intensive but well worth the effort.

The Ingredients:
- *lentils, turmeric (or curry powder), thyme, vegetable (or chicken) broth, coconut oil, yellow onion, lemongrass paste, salt, cardamom, cinnamon, red pepper flakes, nutmeg, coconut milk, Swiss chard (or kale/spinach), lemon (or lime or orange juice), cilantro*

The Recipe:

- Mix in a large soup pot 1½ cups rinsed green lentils, 1½ tsp. turmeric (or curry powder), 2 tsp. dried thyme (or 1 tbsp. fresh thyme leaves), 4 cups vegetable (or chicken) broth.
- Bring lentil mixture to a boil, reduce heat and simmer – covered for 20 minutes.
- While lentils cook sauté in a skillet 1 tbsp. coconut oil with 1 large diced yellow onion until brown.
- Add 2-3 tbsp. lemongrass paste (sold in produce section), 1 tsp. salt, ½ tsp. cardamom, ½ tsp. cinnamon, pinch of red pepper flakes, pinch of nutmeg and sauté for another minute.
- Add the sautéed onion mixture to the cooked lentils and stir keeping heat on low or low simmer.
- Add 1¼ cup of full fat coconut milk and a few handfuls of Swiss chard, kale or spinach and simmer for an additional 5 minutes until greens are wilted.
- Finish with 3 tbsp. lemon, lime or orange juice.
- Serve warm, sprinkling toasted flake coconut and cilantro on top.

Adjustments:

Although, as can be seen, the recipe already includes several options. Other possibilities include using low fat coconut milk and substituting chopped cashews for flake coconut. Experiment and enjoy.

Quick Oriental Soup

This quick and easy soup comes to us via Anne and Mary, from the Flossmoor kitchens of Cath and John Berg. During any visit to their home, one could expect not only the most gracious hospitality but delights to eat. This is an example.

The Ingredients:
- *chicken broth, canned chicken noodle soup, package of frozen oriental vegetables, shredded cooked chicken, green onions, lemon*

The Recipe:
- *Simmer in a large pot 2 cans chicken broth, 1 can chicken noodle soup, 1½ cup water, 1 16 oz. package of frozen Oriental vegetables until vegetables are tender.*
- *Add 1½ cup of shredded cooked chicken.*
- *Heat thoroughly.*
- *Serve hot, garnished with 2 tbsp. diagonally sliced green onions and a lemon peel.*

Adjustments:
To add the bit more Oriental flavor, Robert suggests adding a couple of drops of soy sauce and dropping a well scrambled egg into the soup as it is cooking allowing it to solidify, not unlike a poached egg.

Cath, Eian, Sean, Mary, Lauren, Billy - treats in Flossmoor

Deviled Hamburgers

Apparently this recipe originated with the Girl Scouts many years ago and, not surprisingly, made its way into Mom's recipe box. Unfortunately, the card seems to have disappeared, or perhaps it was worn out from use. When the ingredients were available, this was a luncheon recipe that most of us learned to cook without too much assistance from Mom… although as we all know, Mom was always ready with advice. Joan tells us that it was one of the lessons at Girl Scout cooking school conducted at the Fort Wayne Public Library.

The Ingredients:
- *ground beef, chili sauce, prepared mustard, dried minced onions, salt, pepper, bread, Worcestershire sauce*

41

The Recipe:
- *Mix in large bowl 1 lb. ground beef, 1/3 cup chili sauce, 1 tsp. prepared mustard (French's), 1½ tsp. Worcestershire sauce, 1 tbsp. dried minced onions, dash of salt and dash of pepper.*
- *Spread thinly on bread/bun and broil until cooked.*
- *Serve hot.*

Adjustments:
This recipe is fairly basic requiring few adjustments, however we seem to recall that on would not go astray adding a bit extra dried minced onions. In addition, placing the concoction directly onto bread could leave the finished product a bit mushy so toasting the bread first was one solution. Finally, finely chopped fresh onion will work in place of dried minced onions.

Avocado Tortilla Soup

Joe modestly claims that he is not really a chef but enjoys messing about in the kitchen and coming up with interesting concoctions. That is the start to becoming a fine chef which will hold him in good stead when, and if, he acquires a life partner. In the meanwhile, he offers this Avocado Tortilla Soup as one such concoction.

The Ingredients:
- *olive oil, cabbage, yellow onion, jalapeño pepper, garlic, black beans, cilantro, cumin, salt, pepper, tortilla chips, avocado*

The Recipe:

- *Heat ¼ cup olive oil in a large frying pan.*
- *Cook 3 cups thinly sliced cabbage, 1 sliced medium yellow onion, 1 sliced dry jalapeno, 1-2 garlic cloves, minced. Sauté until cabbage begins to brown.*
- *Pour 4 cups chicken stock into frying pan, de-glazing the pan.*
- *Add ½ can black beans, 2-3 stalks of cilantro, dash of cumin, dash of salt, dash of pepper (to taste) and simmer for 3-5 minutes.*
- *Place a layer of thick tortilla chips on the bottom of soup bowls and ladle soup over the chips.*
- *Garnish with sliced avocado.*

Joe - it's all in the presentation

Better Butter Burgers

Doesn't everything taste better with butter? As if burgers were not high enough in fats, Joe presents this recipe as proof that nothing can be too tasty or unhealthy. We would not suggest making this meal a regular luncheon feast, although, perhaps after enjoying one too many MI Dark and Stormys the night before, it might be just the tonic.

The Ingredients:
- *ground beef, butter, mayonnaise, soy sauce, brown sugar, garlic, blue cheese pepper, Worcestershire sauce, milk, lettuce, shallots*

The Recipe:
- *Crumble 2 lbs. 70/30 ground beef (or the highest fat ratio available) into a mixing bowl.*
- *Pour 3 tbsp. melted butter over the ground beef and mix by hand.*
- *Form beef into 4 loosely packed patties and indent the middle with a spoon-sized dimple.*
- *Sprinkle salt on patties and refrigerate.*
- *Whisk together, in a small bowl, ¾ cup mayonnaise, 2 tbsp. soy sauce, 1 tbsp. Worcestershire sauce, 1 tbsp. brown sugar, 1 clove minced garlic, ¾ tsp. pepper and refrigerate.*
- *Fry 2 chopped shallots in veggie oil and set on kitchen paper to cool.*
- *Heat skillet with a bit of oil on high until it is almost smoking.*
- *Cook patties for 5 minutes on each side.*

- *Top patties with crumbled blue cheese and place under pre-heated broiler for 3 minutes.*
- *Serve on toasted buns assembling burgers topped with shallots, lettuce (Boston bibb or red leaf recommended) and mayonnaise mixture sauce.*

Bean Pasta and Greens Soup

This soup comes to us from Nick; which Cait assures us is the best chicken noodle soup ever. Although it does not originate with Nick, but rather his mother Rene Safley, the fact that it has made its way into Nick's kitchen, bodes well for his culinary appreciation. That would be a vital requirement for admission into the extended Connolly clan.

The Ingredients:
- *olive oil, garlic, fresh spinach (or chard or kale), chicken stock (or beef or vegetable) salt, Parmesan cheese, onion, chick peas (or beans), pasta, pepper, chicken*

The Recipe:
- *Sauté 1 finely chopped onion until brown in 2 tbsp. olive oil in a large frying pan.*
- *Stir in 2 cloves minced garlic and ¼ tsp. dried rosemary.*
- *Add 1 lb. fresh spinach (or chard or kale) and cook on medium heat for about 5 minutes.*
- *Add 1 can (2 cups) chick peas (or beans) and 6 cups chicken stock (or beef or vegetable) and simmer over medium heat.*

- *Add 1 cup pasta and cubed chicken (if desired) and cook, stirring occasionally until pasta is tender.*
- *Season with ¼ tsp. salt and dash of pepper.*
- *Serve with ½ cup grated Parmesan (if desired).*

Cait - of course I love mush!

No Cream* Creamy Broccoli Soup

Kasey presents her specialty with the caveat, "Everything is better with a bit of cream," so it is always added at the end. We could not agree more. Heathy is one thing but let us not go overboard. This excellent soup provides the right mix of healthy and hearty ingredients with warmth against a chill.

The Ingredients:

- *carrots, celery, onions olive oil, chicken (or vegetable) broth (regular or reduced sodium), pepper, broccoli florets, minute rice (brown is preferred but white will do) milk, Parmesan, *cream*

The Recipe:

- *Sauté 1 medium chopped onion, 1 cup chopped carrots and 1 cup chopped celery in a large sauce pan using 3 tbsp. olive oil over medium-high heat for 5 minutes.*
- *Add 2 14.5 oz. cans regular or reduced sodium chicken (or vegetable) broth and bring to a boil.*
- *Stir in ½ cup minute rice (brown preferred) and 4½ cups broccoli florets.*
- *Reduce heat to medium-low, simmer for 15 minutes or until vegetables are tender, stirring frequently.*
- *Add soup in small batches to a blender or food processor, cover, and then blend until pureed.*
- *Return soup puree to saucepan.*
- *Add 2 cups milk, ¼ cup grated Parmesan and ¼-½ cup cream* if desired.*
- *Cook at low heat until heated thoroughly, stirring occasionally.*
- *Season with salt and pepper, if desired, and serve hot.*

John and Kasey – serious cooking

Salmon Burgers

Another blossoming chef, Eian, checks in with his specialty, salmon burgers. Eian delivers the recipe with the caveat that the amounts listed are a bit difficult to pin down because, he usually, "plays it by ear." This is great news because we all know playing it by ear is the best way to cook most things. Strict adherence to a recipe might be fine, but a bit of freelancing, not too much mind you, can transform a meal into something special.

The Ingredients:
- *salmon, parmesan cheese, egg, onion, bell peppers, lemon juice, cayenne pepper flakes, red pepper flakes, saltine crackers, mayonnaise, red wine vinegar, horseradish, honey, butter, olive oil, cashews, Hawaiian buns*

The Recipe:

- *In a small bowl create a sauce mixing 2 dollops mayonnaise, 1 tbsp. horseradish, 2 tbsp. red wine vinegar and a swirl of honey and put aside.*
- *Dice ½ a medium onion and chop one small, red, yellow and orange bell peppers and mix in large bowl.*
- *Add 2 5 oz. packages of cooked boneless pink salmon, crumbled.*
- *Stir in 1 egg, 1 dollop mayonnaise, 3 tbsp. lemon juice, ¼ cup parmesan.*
- *Add dash of cayenne pepper and red pepper flakes and mix.*
- *Add about 5 crushed saltine crackers and mix again.*
- *Wash hands and then roll salmon mix into balls of desired size.*
- *In a large skillet, melt 2 tbsp. butter and add 2 tbsp. olive oil. Place salmon ball in skillet and flatten into patties.*
- *Cook one side for about 10 minutes or until bottom is darkened. Flip and repeat process on second side*
- *Serve on Hawaiian buns topping with mayo/horseradish sauce.*

Macaroni And Cheese

Macaroni and Cheese has been a favorite lunch (or dinner), for generations of Connollys and it is clear that the tradition is not likely to end soon. While the Mac and Cheese served at 4305 was fairly basic, the next generation has taken it to a whole new gourmet level. These recipes are courtesy of Lauren, who tells us that the Spicy Roasted Vegetable is the one she serves most often.

Spicy Roasted Vegetable Mac and Cheese

The Ingredients:
- *broccoli, red pepper, yellow squash, carrots, whole wheat pasta, olive oil, garlic, all-purpose flour, milk, Sargento shredded sharp cheddar cheese, red pepper flakes, cayenne pepper, salt, pepper, Panko breadcrumbs*

The Recipe:
- *In a mixing bowl, toss 1 cup broccoli florets chopped into small chunks, ½ medium red pepper diced, 1 medium yellow squash quartered and diced, 10 baby carrots.*
- *Spread vegetables on a large baking sheet lined with aluminum foil and coated with a bit of olive oil or non-stick cook spray.*
- *Bake in oven pre-heated to 400° F. for 20 minutes or until vegetables have softened.*
- *Boil a medium pot of salted water, lower heat slightly and cook 2 cups of whole wheat pasta according to package instructions. Drain and set aside.*
- *Heat ¼ cup of olive oil in a large skillet and once hot, sauté 1 minced clove of garlic for 30 seconds.*
- *Whisk in 3 tbsp. all-purpose flour and cook for 1 minute.*
- *Gradually whisk in 1½ cup milk until mixture is slightly thickened and then remove from heat.*
- *Stir in 2 cups Sargento shredded sharp cheddar until it is well distributed and melted.*

- *Stir in ½ tsp. crushed red pepper flakes, ½ tsp. cayenne pepper, salt and pepper to taste.*
- *Add baked vegetables and cooked macaroni and blend.*
- *Place entire mixture in a large casserole dish and sprinkle with panko breadcrumbs.*
- *Cook under broiler (500° F.) for 3-4 minutes or until top is golden brown.*
- *Serve hot.*

Adjustments:

Lauren suggests making a double batch which fits perfectly into a 9x12 baking dish and allows plenty for leftovers or delivering to a "bring a dish" function. Typically, Lauren does not include the breadcrumbs and she suggests that if doubling the recipe not to double the cayenne pepper, particularly since you are also using red pepper flakes. If your diners do not appreciate spice, go easy on the cayenne pepper. Finally, use plenty of oil or the cheese mixture can be a bit dry.

Smoked Gouda Macaroni and Cheese with Bacon

The Ingredients:

- *elbow macaroni, butter, onion, flour, chicken broth, milk, heavy cream, kosher salt, dry mustard, pepper, Worcestershire sauce, smoke Gouda cheese, sharp cheddar cheese, cream cheese, Panko bread crumbs, bacon, Parmesan cheese*

The Recipe:
For the Topping:
- *Combine 2 cups Panko bread crumbs, 4 tbsp. melted butter, 6 slices of bacon –*

cooked crispy and crumbled, and ½ cup Parmesan cheese.

For the Macaroni:
- Cook 16 oz. elbow macaroni according to the package instructions.
- In a large, oven-safe pan, melt 4 tbsp. butter and sauté 1 medium diced onion until translucent and just starting to brown.
- Reduce heat to medium and whisk in ½ cup flour until well-mixed and then cook for one minute.
- Combine 1½ cup milk, 1¼ cup heavy cream in a large measuring cup and then add to onion/flour all at once, whisking over medium heat for 1-2 minutes until the mixture thickens considerably.
- Add 2 tsp. kosher salt, 1 tsp. ground black pepper, 1 tsp. dry mustard and 2 tsp. Worcestershire sauce and continue to cook for 2-3 minutes.
- Add ½ lb. shredded smoked Gouda cheese and ½ cup shredded sharp cheddar cheese and stir to combine.
- Reduce heat to low, add cooked macaroni and cook for 5 minutes allowing everything to melt together and heat up. Then smooth the top of the concoction.
- Sprinkle topping on macaroni/cheese mixture.
- Cook under broiler until the top starts to brown.
- Remove and serve hot.

Adjustments:
This recipe can be prepared in advance reserving the topping which is added just before the dish is

put under the broiler and finished. Lauren generally doesn't double this recipe…except for the bacon….and will frequently dispense with the breadcrumbs.

Connollys in the Kitchen: Then and Now, 2016

SIDES AND SALADS

 No dinner would be complete without a few interesting side dishes and/or salads. When the gang was growing up, Mom was a strong believer in meat/fish, potato/rice, and vegetable at each meal. While that might sound 'routine' she was always on the lookout for recipes to spice things up and generally, those ideas were well received. We would be remiss, however, if we did not mention one recipe which made it to the table once, and was never repeated....garden peas cooked in orange juice...yuk. Of course at holidays and on special occasions the sides/salads became - and continue to be – more elaborate. In this section we will explore the most popular side dishes and salads.

Twice Baked Potatoes

This recipe originates with Aunt Cath and is a particularly sinful way to maximize caloric intake when enjoying a steak. One of the particular pleasures of visiting Cath in the days when she was healthy was the opportunity to enjoy a wonderful meal...often steak or lobster... at a dinner which might last for well over an hour. There are some members of our family who insist that such delicacies were reserved for certain people, apparently the 'Royal Couple' comes to mind, but perhaps limitations were the result of larger groups of family members arriving and/or Cath getting on in years.

The Ingredients:
- *potatoes, butter, sour cream, Tabasco sauce, (optional: cheddar cheese, bacon bits, paprika, chives)*

The Recipe:
- *Oven bake an appropriate number of potatoes, (Idaho or Jacket) in the normal way.*
- *Once baked, split the potatoes lengthwise and scoop out the insides mashing them in a bowl. Add plenty of butter and sour cream and a dash of Tabasco sauce.*
- *Place the skins in an aluminum foil boat -1 per boat.*
- *Return the mashed concoction to the skins.*
- *Bake the potatoes a second time for about 20 minutes at 350° F.*

Adjustments:
Although the recipe is for "twice baked" Cath would sprinkle parmesan cheese and broil the potatoes as the final step. Other options include sprinkling paprika on the potato boat before the second bake for a bit of color and flavor; Try adding chives and/or bacon bits to the concoction. Alternatively, sprinkle a bit of cheddar cheese over the potatoes before the second bake. These potatoes can be frozen for future use after the boats are prepared and before the second bake.

Chinese Chicken Salad

This recipe comes from June Murphy's kitchen. Some years ago Robert and Mom attended the wedding of Matt and Amy Murphy and the reception was held at Uncle Pat and Aunt Nan's home in Escondido. As with many West Coast Murphy affairs, it was a bit different...cigars, ties on the head, etc. etc. but for purposes of this book, the guests brought dishes and this one was extremely popular. June, who is married to Uncle Pat's son Mike, provided this salad. It has now been introduced into Ireland where the natives are very impressed. Thank you June.

The Ingredients:
- *vegetable oil, vinegar, sugar, salt, pepper, cabbage, carrots, red cabbage, Ramen noodles, black sesame seeds, almonds, chives, chicken breasts (or chicken-style quorn)*

The Recipe:
- *Mix ¾ cup vegetable oil, 1/3 cup seasoned white wine vinegar, ¼ cup sugar, 1 tsp. salt and 1 tsp. pepper in a dressing jar. Shake thoroughly to ensure sugar is dissolved.*
- *Mix 1 lb. shredded cabbage, ¼ cup grated carrots, ½ cup grated red cabbage, 2 3 oz. packages of Ramen noodle soup (crumbled), 3 tsp. black sesame seeds, 1 cup slivered toasted almonds, 1½ cup chopped chives, 2 or 3 baked chicken breasts, sliced/chopped.*
- *Add dressing to cabbage salad and chill for at least 1 hour, stirring occasionally.*

Adjustments:
If you are serving a number of people, it is recommended that you double the recipe and it

will disappear quickly. In Ireland, we have used chicken quorn bits flash fried in a wok with a bit of soy sauce instead of chicken. The quorn allows for a longer refrigerator life if there are leftovers. Doubling the recipe, even for a smaller crowd, means lunch for at least a few days....eaten with chopsticks of course. The sesame seeds used are black and one can add at least a couple more teaspoons. Obviously, if dealing with an aversion to nuts, the almonds can be eliminated. Hopefully, your garden produces plenty of chives as quite a large quantity is required for this recipe.

Taco Salad

Sticking with the ethnic theme we move on to this popular favorite. Although Mexican food was a bit exotic, Mom undoubtedly discovered this recipe, perhaps on the back of a Frito's corn chip bag, and served it on occasion as a dinner dish.

The Ingredients:
- *ground beef, Frito's corn chips, Hidden Valley Ranch dressing, Miracle Whip, sour cream, kidney beans, iceberg lettuce, cheddar cheese*

The Recipe:
- *Mix 1 package Hidden Valley Ranch dressing, 1 cup Miracle Whip, 1 cup sour cream and refrigerate.*
- *Brown 1 pound, ground beef/chuck then cool.*
- *Mix 1 large head of shredded iceberg lettuce, 1 can drained kidney beans, 8 oz.*

shredded cheddar cheese and the cooled beef.
- *Stir in dressing at least an hour before serving.*
- *Serve over a bed of Frito's corn chips.*

Adjustments:
Some people prefer to eliminate the kidney beans while some people add chopped green onions and/or diced tomatoes. Ground chuck or round steak can replace the ground beef and using different cheese, jack for example, adds a different flavor. A bit of chili or cayenne pepper might also be considered.

Sean - never too young to chop

Potato Casserole

This recipe was perfected by Joan nearly twenty years ago and has been her 'go to' side when providing potluck at family gatherings. Although she will admit it isn't quite Twice Baked Potatoes, it is excellent none the less.

The Ingredients:
- *hash brown potatoes, canned potato soup, canned celery soup, sour cream, cheddar cheese, parmesan (or breadcrumbs)*

The Recipe:
- *Mix 2 packages of frozen hash brown potatoes, 1 can potato soup, 1 can celery soup, 8 oz. sour cream, 8 oz. shredded cheddar cheese and place in baking pan.*
- *Sprinkle parmesan cheese or breadcrumbs on top.*
- *Bake at 350° F. for 1 hour.*

Adjustments:
Some people prefer to replace the potato and celery soups with cream of mushroom soup, adding a different taste.

Scandinavian Cucumbers

Mom undoubtedly discovered this recipe somewhere along the line when Dad's garden produced an abundance of cucumbers…and what would one do with all those cucumbers? This salad provides an excellent accompaniment to al fresco dining, particularly on warm summer evenings.

The Ingredients:
- *sour cream, sugar, parsley, vinegar, onion, dill weed, cucumbers*

The Recipe:

- *Mix ½ cup sour cream, 1 tbsp. sugar, 2 tbsp. parsley, 2 tbsp. vinegar, 1 tbsp. finely chopped onion, ¼ tsp. dill weed.*
- *Stir together and fold in 3 cups thinly sliced cucumbers.*
- *Chill for at least two hours before serving.*

Adjustments:

This rather straightforward recipe is not subject to significant adjustment however it can be served as a condiment as well as a salad as it is very light and refreshing.

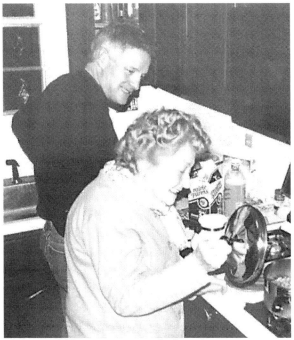

John and Mom - everyone's favorite...green peas

Stuffed Mushrooms

Most of the Connolly family have been big fans of mushrooms which are included in a number of recipes or can accompany others. With its damp climate, Ireland seems to be an ideal place to grow mushrooms and they are readily available, in many varieties, all year round. Pamela and Robert have developed this recipe, and variations thereon to serve with our "go-to" grilling specialty, steak and twice baked potatoes.

The Ingredients:
- *mushrooms, butter, garlic, thyme, lemon juice, breadcrumbs, Parmesan, salt, pepper*

The Recipe:

- *Broil lightly, 16 open-cap mushrooms, with the stems removed, upside down with a small bit of butter on the back of the mushrooms to melt into mushrooms.*
- *Place mushroom caps into a pan/aluminum foil, cap side up.*
- *Mix ¼ cup softened butter 3 cloves pressed garlic, 2 tbsp. fresh thyme, 1½ tbsp. lemon juice, the mushroom stems –chopped, a dash of salt and a dash of pepper and spoon into mushroom caps.*
- *Press ¼ cup of breadcrumbs combined with a sprinkling of grated Parmesan into caps.*
- *Bake at 350° F. for 10 minutes*

Adjustments:
There are a variety of adjustments available depending on taste. One adjustment includes adding blue cheese or crab meat to the butter mixture, leaving out the breadcrumbs altogether and grilling the mushrooms under the broiler instead of baking. Large mushroom caps are best but there is certainly nothing wrong with using portabellos or any more exotic mushroom.

Anne and John - hard at work

Turkey Stuffing

Mom passed the recipe and "assignment" for the Thanksgiving Turkey Stuffing on to Anne and Sheila. This recipe serves 10-20. Family "hold back" if necessary. The big problem was/is keeping some of the boys from eating the stuffing before it made it into the turkey or onto the dinner table. In the earlier years, the stuffing was actually stuffed into the turkey, with the leftovers warmed and served separately. Later, it was decided that having spent time inside the cooking bird, it was a bit too moist and glumpy. Hence the "stuffing" was omitted and served separately. As you can see below, after years of experimentation, Sheila has developed her own techniques so we will use her recipe.

Sheila's Version

The Ingredients:
- *Pepperidge Farm sandwich bread, turkey liver, butter, onions, celery, thyme, flour, salt, pepper*

The Recipe:

Before the Big Day:

- *Two to three days ahead of time, cut 2 loaves of Pepperidge Farm sandwich bread (regular slices) into small cubes and place into large bowls, cake pans or onto cookie trays to dry out. A large, clean, brown paper bag also works well for drying purposes and makes for easy transportation, should you be traveling.*
- *Toss, turn or shake bread cubes frequently to ensure all get dry.*
- *The day before, (Leave the celery and on-ion chopping for the day of only if you have time and helpers.) dice into small cubes 8 stalks of celery and refrigerate in a plastic bag or container.*
- *Dice 1 large onion into small pieces and place in a tightly sealed container. A plastic bag has been used, but somehow the*

64

whole refrigerator ends up smelling like onions. :)

-

<u>On the Big Day:</u>

- *Divide the bread cubes and celery into two large bowls.*
- *Lightly season the turkey liver with flour, salt and pepper.*
- *Melt half a stick of butter in a medium frying pan and cook the liver in the butter. When it is completely cooked, remove from heat and cool.*
- *Cut liver into small pieces and add to the bread and celery.*
- *In the same frying pan, melt the other half a stick of butter and sauté half of the onions and pour over one bowl of bread cubes.*
- *Melt another stick of butter and sauté the rest of the onions and add to the stuffing mixes.*
- *After mixing all the main ingredients: bread, celery, onion, liver and BUTTER, begin to season to taste with salt and thyme.*
- *Begin tasting. There is no limit to the amount of input from various tasters. However, John usually has the last word.*
- *Once all tasters agree that the stuffing is perfect, cover tightly with aluminum foil and put in a safe, cool place - a cooler, garage, car.... The harder it is for John and others to find, the more there will be to put in the oven and have for dinner.*
- *The stuffing gets oven time after the turkey comes out. No set time, just in for warming and a bit of crisping on top.*

Adjustments:

Unfortunately, Pepperidge Farm bread is not universally available so something else might have to do. Some have experimented with whole wheat or other types of bread which adds a different twist. If you forget to stale the bread naturally, put slices under the broiler for a few minutes but not until it is toasted.

John, Pat and Mom - preparing the Thanksgiving feast

Candied Yams/Sweet Potatoes

We are not quite sure where this recipe originated, probably from Joan as only someone of her girth would have the temerity to present such a sinful concoction. It has, however, made its way onto the menu for Christmas and Thanksgiving on both sides of the Atlantic, meeting with universal acclaim.

The Ingredients:
- *yams/sweet potatoes, butter, sugar, eggs, evaporated milk, vanilla, brown sugar, flour, pecans*

The Recipe:
For the potatoes:
- *Mix 2-3 cans of yams (or 6 lbs. sweet potatoes baked, scooped out and mashed), 1 cup unsalted butter, 1 cup sugar, 4 eggs, 2/3 cup evaporated milk, 2 tsp. vanilla in a mixing bowl.*
- *Spread evenly into a baking dish.*

For the topping:
- *Mix 2 cups brown sugar, 2/3 cup butter, 2/3 cup flour, 2 cups chopped pecans in a mixing bowl.*
- *Sprinkle toping over the potato mix*

Cooking:
- *Bake for 35 minutes in a preheated oven at 375° F.*
- *Serve hot.*

Brussels Sprouts

We do not recall Brussels sprouts making too many appearances at dinner time because Mom did not favor cabbage and its relatives. As they are a tradition in Ireland, and since the Connolly family has expanded back to its ancestral home, this recipe is included. Coincidentally, Robert moved to Ireland in 2001, exactly one hundred years after Gram moved to the United States.

The Ingredients:
- *Brussels sprouts, salt, butter, onions, almond flakes*

The Recipe:
- *Boil 3½ cups of peeled Brussels sprouts and a dash of salt in water for 8-10 minutes.*
- *Immediately remove sprouts from water and spray or submerge in cold water to stop continued cooking.*
- *Before serving, sauté sprouts in butter, a touch of oil and a small bit diced onions.*
- *Sprinkle with toasted almond flakes before serving.*

Adjustments:
If diners have difficulty with nuts...Mary... one can always, like green beans almandine, add almonds after non-nut portions have been removed.

Fried Rice

During a couple of school years living in Glen Ellyn, Robert helped to run a youth center in Chicago's Chinatown and took some cooking lessons from one of the children's mothers. Subsequently, there were occasions at 4305 and Getz Road (where Robert, John and Pat resided for various periods of time) when a Chinese feast was prepared. These were generally massive undertakings, as there could be 15-20 guests, were well received and left the kitchen in bits. Robert directed traffic, John was often the fry chef and Pat the sous chef. During the process their hard labor was softened by a bit of plum wine making the cooking more fun. On one occasion, Pat was seen dancing with Seamus O'Toole, the Irish wolfhound who towered over her. While there are many Chinese recipes available from those days, we will restrict the contribution to fried rice.

The Ingredients:

- *minute rice, peanut oil, boneless pork, scallions, salt, pepper, parsley, soy sauce, bean sprouts, pea pods, water chestnuts, eggs*

The Recipe:

- *At least 2 days before cooking, boil 4 cups of white rice and put the cooked rice aside in a large bowl to allow the starch to dry out of the rice. Stir occasionally.*
- *On cooking day, brown the rice in a wok using 4 tbsp. peanut oil and put aside.*
- *Add a bit more peanut oil to the wok and flash fry 1½ cups pork cut into thin strips, ¾ cups chopped scallions including green stems, 1 tsp. salt, ¼ tsp. pepper, ½ cup finely cut parsley, 2 tbsp. soy sauce, large handful of fresh bean-sprouts, large handful fresh pea pods, and small can of sliced water chestnuts.*
- *Return rice to wok and cook together with all other ingredients adding a bit more soy sauce to flavor.*
- *Before serving, make a hole in the rice at the base of the wok and add 2 beaten eggs. Stir the eggs…like scrambled… and when they begin to firm up, mix them into the entire dish.*

Adjustments:

Fried rice is a very flexible dish and can be cooked with chicken, shrimp or no meat/fish at all. In addition, peanut oil is not the healthiest of oil options, although possibly the tastiest, so other oils can also be used. Irish rapeseed oil burns at a high temperature and is an ideal and healthy alternative for stir-fry. Finally, other available vegetables including peas and mushrooms are excellent additions. The most important part of the recipe is drying the starch off the rice or it will stick together making frying difficult.

Coleslaw

Mom's coleslaw was very basic and that is the recipe we will start with. Over the years, although the main ingredients, cabbage and carrots remain the same, this dish has been subject to any number of adjustments.

The Ingredients:
- *cabbage, carrots, Miracle Whip*

The Recipe:
- *Chop green/white cabbage in whatever amount required.*
- *Add carrot peels using a potato peeler.*
- *Add Miracle Whip to desired consistency.*
- *Refrigerate and serve chilled.*

Adjustments:
Some people prefer mayonnaise or salad cream to Miracle Whip. Others add, to a large head of chopped cabbage, 1/3 cup sugar, ¼ cup vinegar, ½ tsp. Cajun Spice, ¼ tsp. black pepper and seasoned salt to taste. Others have experimented with a bit of red cabbage, along with green pepper and the carrots, or perhaps crushed pineapple.

The slaw can be supplemented with poppy seeds or celery seeds. Connolly chefs should always be encouraged to experiment.

Sheila and Linda – perfect salads

Broccoli Salad

Having purchased broccoli salad at a salad bar on one too many occasions, Robert decided that he could produce a more than acceptable alternative. As with many salads, one is encouraged to experiment with ingredients.

The Ingredients:
- *fresh broccoli, salad cream, bacon bits, raisins, peanuts*

The Recipe:
- *Chop broccoli florets into bite sized bits eliminating substantial parts of the stems.*
- *Mix with salad cream, raisins and bacon bits (to taste).*
- *Refrigerate until ready to use.*
- *Before serving, add dry-roasted salted peanuts.*
- *Serve chilled.*

Adjustments:
Miracle Whip is certainly an alternative to salad cream and craisins can replace raisins. Some people like a bit of green onion. The peanuts and bacon bits are also optional. Cauliflower bits or carrot peels add color variety. Experiment with tastes you enjoy keeping in mind how healthy fresh broccoli and/or cauliflower are for you.

Summer Pasta Salad

This recipe was undoubtedly plucked from some magazine because it sounded interesting to Mom, and of course, she was correct. The recipe has travelled well across the Atlantic and it is a go-to salad for al fresco presentations on the deck in Raheny. The staff of Collinstown Park Community College, where Pamela teaches, typically enjoys this treat on "potluck" days, albeit with gluten-free pasta. Of course it is necessary to smuggle McCormick's Supreme Salad Seasoning into Ireland but a bottle doesn't weigh much. Julie also presents a similar salad using linguini pasta. The essential differences are included in the *Adjustments* below.

The Ingredients:
- *spaghetti, McCormick's Supreme Salad Seasoning, cucumber, canned corn, green peppers, tomatoes, Paul Newman's Own Italian Dressing*

The Recipe:
- *Boil one package of spaghetti, drain and cool.*
- *Mix in one small bottle of McCormick's Supreme Salad Seasoning, refrigerate over-night.*
- *Mix into pasta several diced tomatoes, 1-2 cucumbers-skinned, sliced and quartered, one small can of corn, 1 cup of diced green peppers and return to refrigerator.*
- *One hour before serving add Paul Newman's Own Italian Dressing and toss.*
- *Return to refrigerator and serve cold.*

Adjustments:
Pamela regularly uses this recipe with gluten free spaghetti which requires a bit different handling. Pamela breaks the spaghetti in half and places it in a large pot. She then pours boiling water over the spaghetti, cooking until the water turns white. The spaghetti is then strained and returned to the pot covered with more boiling water and again brought to the boil. After turning off the heat, the spaghetti sits for about 5 minutes before again straining and rinsing with cold water to halt further cooking. Finally, she uses red, yellow and orange sweet peppers, as well as green, for a bit more

color. The amount of vegetables added depends a great deal on the cook.

Julie's Linguini Salad: *Julie eliminates the overnight preparation by mixing all the ingredients, adding 1 medium chopped onion and 1 can sliced ripe olives, refrigerating and serving chilled.*

Joan and Anne – please don't add orange juice to those peas

Canarian Potatoes

This recipe enters the Connolly family through Pamela who originally acquired it in the Canary Islands, believe it or not. By way of a bit of trivia, the Canaries, a Spanish protectorate off the west coast of Africa, are not named after the small yellow bird with an identical name, rather it comes from the Romans. In Latin, Insula Canaria means Island of the Dogs. These potatoes, however, have nothing to do with dogs or birds, but are a simple and pleasant alternative to baked or boiled new potatoes, particularly in warmer weather.

The Ingredients:
- *soft skinned potatoes, oil, sea salt*

The Recipe:
- *Wash a bag of small soft skinned potatoes (new potatoes).*
- *Spread, uncut, on microwaveable plate and coat well with ground sea-salt.*
- *Microwave at high heat for about 7 minutes or until soft. (For a large number of potatoes it may be necessary to nuke in batches.)*
- *Place potatoes in baking pan and bake at 400° F. for 20-30 minutes or until potatoes are toasty brown. During the cooking process shake the tray frequently to rotate potatoes.*
- *Serve hot.*

Apple Cashew Salad

Julie presents this specialty from her collection of treats and, not surprisingly, we are tempted to try it out immediately.

The Ingredients:
- *olive oil, red wine vinegar, onion, poppy seeds, dry mustard, sugar, salt, romaine lettuce, granny smith apples, Swiss cheese, cashews, croutons*

The Recipe:
For the Dressing
- *Mix in bowl/bottle ½ cup olive oil, 3 tbsp. red wine vinegar, 1 tbsp. grated onion, 2*

tbsp. poppy seeds, 1 tsp. dry mustard, ¼ cup sugar, ½ tsp. salt.

<u>For the Salad</u>

- *Mix in large bowl 1 head romaine lettuce, 1 Granny Smith apple - chopped, 4 oz. (or more) grated Swiss cheese and 8 oz. cashews.*
- *Drizzle dressing onto salad and toss.*

John, Mom, Joan, Pat, Jack – summer salads
(and Jack has a bottle of Dempseys)

Casa Style Salad

Casa D'Angelo is a well-known and very popular Italian restaurant group in Fort Wayne. Casa's is famous for its salad but the recipe is a closely guarded secret. This salad is Julie's take on de-engineering the ingredients and we would certainly agree that it closely resembles the original...and is far less expensive.

The Ingredients:
- *anchovies, red wine vinegar, oregano, pepper, salt, sugar, garlic, cornstarch, olive oil, lettuce (romaine, iceberg), pimentos (or diced red peppers), onion, mozzarella/ romano cheese*

The Recipe:
For the Dressing
- *In a small bowl mix 6 chopped anchovies, 8 oz. red wine vinegar, ¾ tsp. oregano, 1½ tsp. pepper, 2-3 tsp. salt, 3 tbsp. sugar, 1½ tsp. garlic (fresh or powder), ¼ cup cornstarch 16 oz. olive oil.*

For the Salad
- *Mix in large bowl variety of lettuce (romaine, iceberg, etc.), 1-2 tbsp. pimentos or diced red pepper, ¼ cup chopped red onion, shredded mozzarella/romano cheese to taste, croutons.*
- *Drizzle dressing onto salad and toss.*

Winter Potatoes

Ireland provides a wide range of potato species for use in a variety of recipes. Pamela has perfected this recipe as an alternative to roast potatoes and it has become a staple for winter meals, including Christmas dinner. The potatoes used in this recipe are typically white or red with a soft skin which is not removed.

The Ingredients:
- *potatoes, olive oil, salt, herbs (any available on spice rack), fresh rosemary, garlic*

The Recipe:
- *Wash and quarter/cut into chunks 1 small bag of potatoes or enough to serve guests expected.*
- *Coat potatoes in olive oil and spread into baking tray/pan.*
- *Sprinkle with sea salt, herbs de provence/mixed herbs, thyme, rosemary, and if fresh rosemary is available put several sprigs among the potatoes.*
- *Add garlic cloves spread among the potatoes.*
- *Bake in preheated oven at 350° F. until middle of the potatoes are soft and outsides are crispy.*
- *Shake baking pan frequently to turn and keep the potatoes from sticking, (additional oil may be required).*

Hawaii Salad

This is another salad from Pamela's collection of al fresco treats and is always well received at deck barbecues when the sun shines in Raheny. While Pamela has embraced many of the Connolly recipes which crossed the Atlantic, this originates in Dublin.

The Ingredients:
- *chunk pineapple, celery, cucumber, canned corn, mayonnaise, salt*

The Recipe:
- *Mix in salad bowl 1 can pineapple cut into small chunks (in the USA can of chunk*

pineapple), 5-6 stalks of celery chopped into thin slices, 1 skinned cucumber halved lengthwise and cut into thin slices, 1 can of corn.
- *Add ½ cup of mayonnaise/Miracle Whip and a dash of salt.*
- *Refrigerate for at least 2 hours before serving cold.*

Oven Roasted Asparagus

Dad maintained an asparagus patch in the back yard of 4305 next to the compost heap. While the patch produced an abundance of fresh asparagus in the late spring and early summer, it was not a universally enjoyed vegetable. However, it was part of our healthy dining; it was on our plates; so it was eaten. Remarkably, the taste buds of members of the next generation have 'matured' differently and Sarah presents this as her favorite asparagus recipe.

The Ingredients:
- *asparagus, salt, pepper, olive oil, garlic powder, Parmesan cheese*

The Recipe:
- *Place asparagus in roasting pan and cover in olive oil.*
- *Sprinkle with salt, pepper, garlic powder and Parmesan (if desired).*
- *Roast in oven at 350° F. for about 15 minutes.*
- *Serve hot.*

Michael and Sarah – baked asparagus

Far East Celery

This recipe comes from the amazing kitchen of Cath and her husband, John Berg. Aunt Cath, Dad's sister, remained unmarried for most of her life and visits to the Connolly family home in Flossmoor are treasured memories. Because she didn't travel very often after she retired, imagine our shock when she turned up at the 1984 Chicago Marathon, which John and Mary ran, and announced she was getting married. John Berg, a lifelong friend of Dad and Cath and widower, was the lucky man. Cath was 65 at the time and John was 85. Cath maintained the next seven years were the happiest time of her life. One reason, perhaps, was that John and Cath shared a love of cooking as well as a sweet tooth, properly maintained by John's confectionary talents. This recipe, coming to us via

Anne, is an interesting addition to any cook's slate of vegetable options.

The Ingredients:
- *celery, water chestnuts, can cream of chicken soup, pimentos, butter, almonds, breadcrumbs*

The Recipe:
- *Boil 4 cups of celery cut into 1 in. pieces for about 8 minutes in a small amount of water and then drain.*
- *Mix in a 1 qt. casserole dish, cooked celery, 1 5 oz. can of sliced water chestnuts, 1 can cream of chicken soup, 1 small jar of chopped pimentos.*
- *Slightly brown in a skillet with 2 tbsp. butter, ½ cup of slivered almonds.*
- *Add almonds/butter to ½ cup breadcrumbs and sprinkle over celery mixture.*
- *Bake at 350° F. for 35 minutes and serve as a vegetable.*

Hard Boiled Eggs

Sean asked that this recipe be included although, one would think, it is fairly basic and should be easily sourced in any cook book. The difference, however, is that this is Cath's easy-to-peel hard-boiled egg recipe which makes it unique. Mary passes it on from Cath's instructions.

The Ingredients:
- *eggs*

The Recipe:
- *Place eggs in pan of water 1 inch over the eggs.*
- *Bring water to boil. Allow to boil 1-2 minutes.*
- *Turn off gas/heat, cover pan and set timer for 15 minutes.*
- *Drain eggs, rinse with cold water until eggs are cold.*
- *Dry eggs, put in carton with big **H** on each and refrigerate.*

Deviled Eggs

There are many versions of this treat which was a standard side when Cath would prepare lunch for her visitors. This particularly recipe comes from Pat's kitchen and we present it as a colorful accompaniment to any collection of salads or as part of an al fresco cook-out.

The Ingredients:
- *eggs, Miracle Whip (or mayonnaise), French's mustard, Tabasco, salt, pepper, paprika*

The Recipe:
- *Hard boil eggs. We recommend Cath's version from the previous recipe as it makes peeling easy.*
- *Remove shells and slice eggs in half, lengthwise.*
- *Carefully scoop out yokes and transfer to a mixing bowl.*
- *Mash or puree the egg yokes. Add Miracle Whip (or mayonnaise), French's mustard,*

Tabasco, salt and pepper to taste and desired thickness.
- *Refill egg whites and sprinkle with paprika.*
- *Refrigerate and serve chilled.*

Adjustments:

This recipe is created to the taste of the chef which is the reason specific measurements of Miracle Whip and mustard are not included. A variety of ingredients can be added to the yoke mix including sour cream, pickle juice, horseradish, cayenne pepper, curry powder, etc. so don't be afraid to experiment. For a fancier presentation, use a pastry tube to refill the whites.

Connollys in the Kitchen: Then and Now, 2016

BREADS AND BUNS

 Baking has a long and storied history in the Connolly family. There was a time, believe it or not, when baking bread was a labor of love and wonderful aromas would fill the house. The bread you bought in the stores, except for that purchased in Gram's favorite bakery in Brookfield, was for bulk consumption and not particularly nutritious. Although Mom was the initial baker, particularly of Irish Soda Bread, at some point Dad took over and experimented with various interesting recipes, some excellent and some not so much. When Pat returned from Ireland after her visit in 1970, she was armed with family recipes for treats like scones… although her first efforts were a bit heavy and only rhymed with 'scones'. She did subsequently perfect the art. In recent years, Jack has become the consummate baker and his treats are thoroughly enjoyed at all family functions. Mike McManus, being the family's biggest bread consumer, has also become a baker but since he has one of those machines you just throw everything into and switch a button, eyebrows have been raised…however, with his bulk consumption that is probably necessary. As Kevin knows, because he kept asking, Sean Hayes, our Irish cousin-of-a-cousin, and frequent visitor to his "American cousins," used the word bun to identify a wide range of bakery products; anything

85

from a doughnut, to a pastry, to a Parker House roll to an English muffin. A bit about Sean Hayes and his penchant for buns might be instructive. Mom had a number of second cousins in Cork, which is not surprising because Gram emigrated leaving a number of first cousins behind. Gram, and later Mom remained in contact with these second cousins via letter...definitely not e-mail or Facebook. Among the ones we knew best were four sisters, Monica, Kitty, Ita and Hilda Murphy who lived together in a home in Sundays Well and later Ballincollig, on the Western Road outside of Cork City. Sean is a first cousin of the Murphys from the side not related to us. Sean, a life-long 'Pioneer' - which means the devil drink has never crossed his lips - only eats chicken, French fries, ice cream and buns and drinks orange drink. His visits are great fun altogether and we are happy to call him our cousin.

Mom and Dad – let the baking begin

Irish Soda Bread

What better place to start than with Gram's/Mom's Irish Soda Bread. This recipe was well used around St. Patrick's Day, and on other special occasions. Homemade Irish Soda Bread made its appearance at various events during which the family attempted to civilize Fort Wayneians by introducing them to Irish Culture at the turn of the century…21st that is. More recently, Mary has become the expert so the recipe lives on.

The Ingredients:
- *flour, sugar baking soda, baking powder, cream of tartar, butter, raisins, buttermilk*

The Recipe:
- *Sift into a large bowl 3 cups flour, ¼ cup sugar, 1 tsp. baking soda ½ cup baking powder and ¼ tsp. cream of tartar.*
- *Repeat this sifting three times.*
- *Cut ½ cup butter into mixture with pastry blender.*
- *Add 1½ cup raisins and mix well.*
- *Stir in 1½ cups buttermilk.*
- *Turn dough out onto lightly floured board and knead gently for ½ minute.*
- *Place in greased pan and bake at 350° F. for 45 minutes to an hour.*

Adjustments
Adjustments are not permitted.

Scones

Scones are a distinctively Irish treat frequently served as an afternoon snack known as 'Tea.' They are not a far cry from Irish Soda Bread but they are 'buns' and served individually. This recipe comes from Brendan and Aileen Goggin who live in Montenotte, Cork City. Pat first met this most hospitable couple when she visited Ireland with Gram in 1970. A couple years later, Brendan Goggin (the base generation's third cousin as we share a great-grandmother) and his bride Aileen visited Brookfield and Fort Wayne on their delayed honeymoon. Brendan and Aileen, became this generation's primary contact in Ireland and we have all taken advantage of their hospitality on numerous occasions. Brendan is an expert on the history of Cork; and his guided tours have been extraordinarily educational experiences. A final word about scones: Brendan explains that while many people use a Michelin Guide to judge a restaurant, the better test is the Scone Index. If a restaurant's scones pass scrutiny in taste, texture, consistency, appearance, volume and price the rest of the food will probably be good.

The Ingredients:
- *flour, butter, salt, bread soda, caster sugar, buttermilk*

The Recipe:
- *Sift 8 oz. flour, and ¼ tsp. salt into a mixing bowl.*
- *Chop 1 oz. butter into small pieces and rub into flour.*
- *Add ½ oz. of caster sugar and ¼ tsp. bread soda (free of lumps) and mix well together.*
- *Mix to a loose dough, turn onto a floured board and flatten into a circle about ½ inch in thickness.*

- *Cut the circle into halves, quarter and then in eighths forming triangles.*
- *Place on a greased tin, brush tops with buttermilk and bake at 350° F. for about 20 minutes.*
- *Serve with plenty of whipped butter and preserves. (Strawberry is particularly good.)*

Adjustments:

While one would not like to alter perfection, some people form the scones into round shapes while others add raisins or sultanas for a bit of fruit. Brendan and Aileen often make brown breakfast scones with essentially the same recipe using 4 oz. of unsifted whole meal flour and 4 oz. sifted regular flour. It is definitely a good idea to double the recipe because these delicacies disappear quickly.

Gram, Aileen, Brendan - visiting Brookfield...
problems with the salt shaker

Tea

One might think this is a peculiar place to insert a recipe for tea. One might even wonder why such a recipe is necessary at all. In Ireland, tea is the perfect companion to soda bread or scones and often served in the late afternoon. While throwing a tea bag into a cup of hot water might be quick and easy, it does not do justice to proper tea like those blended by Barry's, our favorite Irish tea. Serving a proper 'cuppa' reflects good breeding and we would not want family members to be caught short in this regard.

The Ingredients:
- *tea, boiling water, sugar (optional), milk or cream (optional)*

The Recipe:
- *Boil water.*
- *Pour boiling water into a proper teapot, warming the pot.*
- *Dump water into sink.*
- *Put teabag(s) into pot and refill with boiling water.*
- *Allow to steep until tea is golden brown.*
- *Serve piping hot.*

Adjustments:
Some people prefer to add milk or cream and/or sugar to their tea which is certainly acceptable. Gram preferred cream or half-and-half. Good practice is to add these ingredients first and then pour the tea into the cup. Carmel Walsh, our cousin from Howth, insists that a proper cuppa uses loose tea, rather than tea bags, in which case it is necessary to employ a tea-ball or tea strainer. As before pour in the boiling water and allow to steep. Enjoy.

90

<u>Old Fashioned White Bread</u>

This recipe is courtesy of Ev Kronawitter, Mom's good friend and Mary's godmother. Undoubtedly, this is a basic recipe dating back to the days when baking bread was a daily occurrence. Pamela's mother told us that she used to bake bread every day and this is the style recipe she, and all our forbearers would use. It would do no harm to give it a try once in a while if, for no other reason, than to have the smell of freshly baked bread wafting through the house.

The Ingredients:
- *dry yeast, sugar, flour, salt*

The Recipe:
- *Mix 1 packet dry yeast and 1 tbsp. sugar in ½ cup of water in a small bowl and let soften.*
- *Sift 6 cups flour and 1 tbsp. salt into large bowl.*
- *Mix in 2 cups warm water, 2 tbsp. oil and yeast mixture.*
- *Add additional flour (not too much) so it no longer sticks to your hands.*
- *Allow the dough to rise until doubled in bulk.*
- *Cut into loaf sized portions and knead for about 3 minutes per loaf then put into greased pans.*
- *Bake at 400° F. for 10 minutes and 350° F. for 35 minutes.*
- *Remove from pans and lay sideways on rack to cool.*

Adjustments:
Every baker has their own recipe and techniques for baking this staple. The important thing is to discover one that works and use it occasionally to remind us all that there was a time when bread was not the sole prerogative of mass bakeries and grocery stores where the natural goodness can be limited by additives and preservatives,

Old Fashioned Brown Bread

This recipe may not be what some people would expect from brown/black bread but it was certainly a treat on evenings when Mom served baked beans. Slathered with butter and/or used to soak up the juice, this bread made such dinners more than acceptable. FYI: in the old days cans were delineated by numbers so when this recipe calls for #303 cans, that would be about 3¼ inches in diameter and 4½ inches high holding about 2 cups. A #300 would be closer to the size of a Campbell's soup can.

The Ingredients:
- *graham/whole wheat flour, all-purpose flour, baking soda, salt, buttermilk, molasses, seedless raisins*

The Recipe:
- *Mix into a large bowl 2 cups graham or whole wheat flour, ½ cup all-purpose flour and 2 tsp. baking soda.*
- *Stir in 1 tsp. salt, 2 cups buttermilk, ½ cup molasses, 1 cup seedless raisins.*
- *Mix well and spoon into 3 well-greased #303 tin cans.*

- *Allow to stand for ½ hour.*
- *Bake at 350° F. for 45-50 minutes or until cake tester (long toothpick) comes out clean.*
- *Cut open bottom of can and gently push bread out.*
- *Slice into ½" to 3/4" pieces; butter and place in broiler for a few minutes. - until edges are crispy. Serve hot.*

Adjustments:
Although we have never experimented, it would theoretically be permissible to use a different size can, adjusting the baking time if the can is smaller (requiring either less batter or more cans). Check with the toothpick to be sure the bread is cooked through. To avoid a kitchen fire, tear the paper label off the can before putting into the oven.

Porridge Brown Bread

In more recent times, Pamela has perfected the art of baking brown bread without any flour. Although there is some question as to whether Quaker oats are completely gluten free, there are rolled oats that certainly are, so this recipe provides a healthy alternative for breakfast or lunch….unless, of course, you slather slices with butter/peanut butter…which is definitely recommended. If you are selling your house, or inviting guests, baking this loaf will produce the most amazing aroma.

The Ingredients:
- *low fat natural yogurt, porridge oats, baking soda, eggs, vanilla, raisins*

The Recipe:
- *Blend into a large bowl 1 large tub (just over 2 cups) low fat natural yogurt with 2 cups porridge oats (use yoghurt tub to ensure equal measure with yoghurt) and 2 tsp. bread (baking) soda.*
- *Beat 2 small eggs and stir thoroughly into oats/yoghurt with a large dash of vanilla essence/extract.*
- *Grease bread tin.*
- *Bake in pre-heated oven at 350° F. for 40 minutes.*
- *Remove loaf from tin, turn over and return loaf to tin, upside down, and bake for another 20 minutes*
- *Remove from oven and tin wrap in tea cloth and place upside down on wire tray to cool.*
- *Cut into slices to freeze for future use.*

Adjustments:
Adding as many raisins as you like transforms this recipe into a nourishing and very tasty breakfast.

Bread Sticks And English Muffins

These recipes use the same dough as Mom's Saturday night pizza, which typically provided more than enough for additional baking.

The Ingredients:
- *dough from Mom's pizza recipe, cornmeal*

The Recipe:
- *Start with excess dough from the Pizza recipe in the Dinner Chapter of this book.*

For Bread Sticks:
- *Roll dough into sticks of preferred size. Cover with towel and allow to double in size.*
- *May be brushed with butter or egg white and sprinkled with seeds or seasonings.*
- *Bake 400º F 10-15 minutes until golden brown.*

For English Muffins:
- *Roll dough to about ¾ inch thickness and, using a large glass or hamburger press cut into round muffin shapes.*
- *Sprinkle bottom of muffins with cornmeal. Cover with towel and allow to double in size.*
- *Cook on an electric skillet or frying pan over medium heat, about 10 minutes on first side, about 5 on second side. Cool.*
- *Use a fork, to perforate around the muffin edges, separate halves, butter and broil muffins when ready to serve.*

Zucchini Bread

Zucchini (known as courgette on the East side of the Atlantic) was another vegetable grown in Dad's garden. Apart from frying slices up with plenty of butter and onions, Mom acquired this recipe from a friend and we were occasionally blessed with this treat. Anne and Mary discovered the recipe among Mom's treasures and passes it on to us.

The Ingredients:
- *eggs, sugar, oil, zucchini, crushed pineapple, flour, salt, baking powder, baking soda, cinnamon, ginger, vanilla, pecans*

The Recipe:
- *Mix in large bowl 3 eggs, 2 cups sugar, 1 cup oil.*
- *Beat until light and fluffy.*
- *Mix in separate bowl 3 cups coarsely shredded zucchini, 8½ can of crushed, drained pineapple.*
- *Add zucchini/pineapple to egg/sugar mixture.*
- *Mix in a separated bowl 3 cups flour, 1 tsp salt, 1 tsp. baking powder, 2 tsp. baking soda, 2 tsp. cinnamon, ½ tsp. ginger, 1 tsp. vanilla.*
- *Slowly stir into egg/zucchini/pineapple mix.*
- *Pour into 2 large or 3 medium greased loaf pans.*
- *Bake at 350º F. for 50 minutes or until toothpick comes out clean.*

Adjustments:
This recipe is actually presented as nut free but it does allow adding 1 cup of chopped pecans to the zucchini and pineapple mixture.

Irish Brown Bread

Perhaps no one in the family has assumed the role as master baker more than Jack. Whether it is a family gathering at Easter, in South Bend, or Christmas in Fort Wayne, or in Monroe for Thanksgiving, Jack delivers an amazing assortment of buns.

rolls and breads. His offerings for this collection are from his Irish baking so they are especially welcome. This recipe makes one loaf, seven inches in diameter.

The Ingredients:

- *all-purpose flour, sugar, baking powder, baking soda salt, butter, whole wheat flour (stone ground if possible), rolled oats, buttermilk*

The Recipe:

- *Combine in mixing bowl 1 cup unsifted all-purpose flour, 2 tbsp. sugar, 1 tsp. baking powder, 1 tsp. baking soda, ½ tsp. salt.*
- *Cut in 1½ tbsp. butter until it reduces to very small particles.*
- *Stir in 2 cups whole-wheat flour (stone-ground if possible) and ¼ cup rolled oats.*
- *Create well in center and add 1½ cups buttermilk, stirring lightly but thoroughly until all flour is moistened.*
- *Turn out onto a lightly floured board.*
- *Knead 5 times.*
- *Gather into a ball and place on lightly greased cookie sheet.*
- *Pat into a 7 inch circle.*
- *Using a sharp knife cut a large cross into the top of the loaf to allow for expansion.*
- *Bake at 375° F. for 35-40 minutes until loaf is brown and sounds hollow when tapped.*
- *Remove from oven and place on wire rack. Brush with melted butter and allow to cool before serving.*

Irish Current Bread

Continuing with his Irish bread theme, Jack presents this specialty which is as much a sweet treat as an ordinary bread. In Ireland, it would be served with afternoon tea, slathered with whipped butter, whipped cream and a berry jam of some description.

The Ingredients:
- currents, milk, Crisco, salt, butter, sugar, cinnamon, nutmeg, eggs, Irish style flour, unbleached all-purpose flour

The Recipe:
- Soak 1 cup currents in ½ cup water.
- Drain well, saving the current soaking water.
- Scald (boil) 1 cup milk and 1 cup water and allow to cool.
- Combine in a large bowl or standing mixer: ½ cup shortening (Crisco), 2 tsp. salt, 1 cup sugar, 1 tsp. cinnamon, ½ tsp. nutmeg.
- Add the cooled milk/water and current water and beat well.
- Stir in 2 well-beaten eggs.
- In a separate bowl stir, 2 scant tbsp. instant yeast, 2 cups Irish style flour (available in King Arthur Flour or by special order from the Royal Couple) and 2 cups unbleached all-purpose flour.
- Add the flour mix to the liquids stirring well.
- Add the drained currents to the dough.
- Add enough Irish Style and all-purpose flour (equal parts) to allow for kneading the dough.

- *Knead by machine or by hand until the dough is a smooth ball.*
- *Place dough in greased bowl, cover with towel and allow to rise for 1½ hours.*
- *Turn onto work surface and divide into three equal portions.*
- *Form each portion into a round loaf.*
- *Allow to rise until almost doubled in size.*
- *Brush loaves with melted butter and sprinkle with 1 tbsp. sugar mixed with ½ tsp. cinnamon.*
- *With a sharp knife slash the tops of the loaves in a cross pattern to allow for further expansion.*
- *Bake at 375° F. for 35-40 minutes until well browned.*
- *Allow to cool before cutting and serving.*

Pat and Jack – a masterpiece

Sweet Potato Muffins

Here is another tasty treat courtesy of Molly and her mother. As we all know, the best recipes are passed down from Mother to daughter/son so one day Caroline with certainly take over. Rumor has it that these "buns" are an annual treat in the Evans household and always disappeared quickly. One would suspect that would also be the case as the recipe has been incorporated into other branches of the family.

The Ingredients:
- *butter, sugar, canned sweet potatoes, baking powder, eggs, all-purpose flour, salt, cinnamon, nutmeg, milk, pecans (or walnuts), raisins*

The Recipe:
- *Melt ½ cup butter and blend with 1¼ cup sugar.*
- *Mix in a bowl the butter/sugar with 2 well beaten eggs.*
- *Blend in 1¼ cups of canned sweet potatoes (yam) well-mashed.*
- *Sift into a separate bowl 1½ cups all-purpose flour, 2 tsp. baking powder, ¼ tsp. salt, 1 tsp. cinnamon, ¼ tsp. nutmeg.*
- *Slowly add the sweet potato mix alternating with 1 cup milk taking care not to overmix.*
- *Fold in ¼ cup chopped pecans (or walnuts) and ½ cup chopped raisins.*
- *Pour into 1½ inch greased muffin tins filling each 2/3 from the top.*
- *Bake at 400° F. for 25 minutes.*

- *Makes about 6 dozen muffins which can be frozen and reheated.*

Caroline - mommy's little helper

Beer Bread

Well we never... This recipe is courtesy of Mike and Mary McManus although it is difficult for us to see Mary enjoying this treat...maybe with a Strawberry Daiquiri. Perhaps it is just the thing to eat with a ham sandwich, a glass of beer and a football game. Mary insists it doesn't taste like beer, but we wouldn't mind if it did.

The Ingredients:
- *flour, baking powder, salt, sugar, beer, butter*

The Recipe:
- *Mix in a bowl 3 cups flour, 3 tsp. baking powder, 1 tsp. salt and ¼ cup sugar.*
- *Blend in 1 can beer (regular or light will do but be sure it is at room temperature…not right out of the fridge) and ¼ cup of melted butter.*
- *Form into loaf and place in a greased bread tin.*
- *Bake at 350° F. for 45 minutes to 1 hour.*

Crusty French Bread

John Berg baked this crusty bread recipes in the kitchen at Flossmoor. We have all enjoyed eating French bread, slathered with garlic butter, with our spaghetti or lasagna, but baking your own, raises the level of deliciousness. The recipe arrives through Anne and Mary.

The Ingredients:
- *bread flour, sugar, active dry yeast, salt, egg*

The Recipe:
- *Mix in a large bowl 2 cups bread flour, 1 tbsp. sugar, 1 package active dry yeast, 3 tsp. salt and 2 cups warm water.*
- *Beat mixture until smooth.*
- *Stir in 3 to 3½ cups bread flour until stiff.*
- *Knead for five minutes adding flour so dough is no longer sticky.*

- *Place dough in a greased bowl and cover with cloth.*
- *Allow to rise until doubled in size (1-1½ hours).*
- *Punch down and shape into one long loaf.*
- *Cover and allow to rise until doubled in size (45 min.).*
- *Combine 1 egg white (slightly beaten) 1 tbsp. water in small bowl and brush on loaf.*
- *Using sharp knife, make three diagonal scores ½ inch deep, across the top of the loaf.*
- *Place loaf on cookie sheet and bake at 375° F. for 40-45 minutes.*
- *Remove and allow to cool on wire rack.*

Dad - baking bread at
4305 McMillen Park Drive

White Potato Bread

In the days before Jack arrived in the family, Dad decided that baking bread was his specialty, apart from the summer grilling. This was particularly true after he retired. Like any kitchen job he undertook, including being the bartender, he was frustrated if anyone got in the way, so the decks had to be cleared before he began baking. That is not to say he didn't appreciate an apprentice. Mary has fond memories of joining Dad in baking White Potato Bread, his go-to recipe, and him explaining the process to her, step by step.

The Ingredients:
- *potatoes, butter, salt, honey, wheat germ, dried yeast*

The Recipe:
- *Peel 2 medium potatoes and bring to the boil in 3 cups water, then allow to simmer for 15 minutes.*
- *Pour off 1 cup of potato water and place in the freezer to cool. Pour the remaining potato water into a large bowl.*
- *Mash the potatoes with ¼ cup butter (room temperature) until smooth.*
- *Add to large bowl with the potato water and mix 1 tbsp. salt, 3 tbsp. honey, ½ cup wheat germ (optional), 1 package dried yeast.*
- *Remove cooled cup of water and add to yeast mix.*
- *Blend yeast mixture and mashed potatoes.*
- *Add 6-8 cups all-purpose flour and knead until dough is smooth and not sticky.*
- *Return dough to greased bowl, cover with towel and let rise for about 1½ hours (allow to double in size).*

- *Punch down and knead a bit more before placing in 2 buttered bread pans. (Save a bit for rolls).*
- *Allow to rise for about 45 minutes or until it doubles again*
- *Bake at 400° F. for 20 minutes (bread) or 10 minutes (rolls) then reduce temperature to 350° F. for 15 minutes.*
- *Allow to cool before serving.*

Connollys in the Kitchen: Then and Now, 2016

CONDIMENTS

 In modern times it is easy enough to head down to the local grocery store and purchase jars or bottles of most any condiment one might need to complement a particular dish. Of course, ketchup and mustard have been with us for a long time but in a bygone era, other more specialized products required a bit of preparation. While one can easily purchase a jar of this or that, preparing these condiments takes very little effort and the end result will be greatly appreciated.

Mint Sauce

Fortunately, there was plenty of mint growing next to the garage at 4305 because it is a vital ingredient for Mint Juleps (see Happy Hour) and, of course, mint sauce served with lamb or lamb chops. This recipe originated with Cath although Mom used a similar recipe.

The Ingredients:
- *confectioner's sugar, mint leaves, vinegar*

The Recipe:
- *Dissolve 1½ tbsp. confectioner's sugar in 3 tbsp. warm water.*
- *Cool this syrup and add 1/3 cup finely chopped mint leaves with ½ cup strong vinegar.*
- *Prepare at least ½ hour before serving allowing flavors to blend.*

Cocktail Sauce

Shrimp would not be the same without cocktail/horseradish sauce. It is really a quite simple recipe but strength depends entirely on the constitution of those who might consume it. Since shrimp cocktail was one of Cath's go-to hors d'oeuvres, we will credit her with the recipe. Later in life, she experimented with "store bought" instead of mixing her own. Although she thought some of these sauces were quite nice, she never objected to our adding more horseradish to liven it up a bit.

The Ingredients:
- *chili sauce, horseradish sauce*

The Recipe:
- *Mix about a cup (depending on number of shrimp) of chili sauce with horseradish sauce to taste....the more horseradish the hotter.*

  Adjustments:
  There are several types of horseradish sauce, available. The purists would use straight horseradish sauce as opposed to the creamed version but, in a pinch, creamed will do. Some people prefer a bit less horseradish adding a splash of Tabasco. Where chili sauce in not

available, or completely different than American chili sauce, (e.g. Ireland) a generic hamburger relish is as close as one can come. Even if chili sauce is available, a red burger relish can add a bit of different texture.

John and Sheila - on the gravy...as usual

Chocolate Sauce

This recipe is courtesy of Cal O'Connor, Kevin's much loved mother who remarked upon meeting Robert for the first time, "Oh, you must be Joan's younger brother!" Since the O'Connor's were also a very large family this was undoubtedly Cal's answer to Mom/Gram's zuzu drizzled over ice cream.

The Ingredients:
- *butter, chocolate, cocoa, sugar, light cream, salt, vanilla*

The Recipe:
- Melt ¼ cup butter and 1 square chocolate in saucepan/double boiler. Stir until smooth
- Mix in a small bowl ¼ cup cocoa, ¾ cup sugar, ½ cup light cream, pinch of salt, 1 tsp. vanilla.
- Stir into chocolate/butter. Serve warm.

Adjustments:
In providing this recipe thirty years ago, Cal said she usually makes at least a double recipe because it keeps well and because Kevin loves it. She also said that margarine is an acceptable substitute for butter, but we really don't see the point.

Chocolate - Chocolate

As one would expect, Mom also had her own version of a chocolate sauce, a staple to enhance ice cream. Tradition has it that Michael would consume massive quantities of vanilla ice cream when he was attempting to bulk up for the Bishop Luers football season. Chocolate – Chocolate Sauce was an ideal supplement. Pat passes this recipe on from her archives with a bit of perspective. Dad was employed by the Department of Agriculture, specifically the Federal Milk Market Administration. At the time, there were dozens of small independent dairies in northern Indiana and his job was to monitor these dairies. Samples of their final package products, including pints, quarts or gallons of milk, cream, half and half, buttermilk, etc., would be delivered to the laboratory in Fort Wayne where they would be tested to ensure they contained the appropriate milk-fat content. This process required only one test tube of product, so the remainder would be disposed of...either down the drain or

110

by the Connolly family. This meant that, quite apart from "Milk Man" home deliveries, (Allen Dairy or Eskay Dairy, on alternate days) there was always plenty of milk to build strong bones. Occasionally, to everyone's delight, Dad would bring home chocolate milk; but Mom's sauce, mixed in white milk, was the next best thing. As a bit of trivia, our second Richard also began his professional career with the Department of Agriculture.

The Ingredients:
- *semi-sweet chocolate, half and half, sugar*

The Recipe:
- *Melt 32 oz. semi-sweet chocolate in a double boiler; then add 1¾ cups sugar and 2½ cups half and half, stirring until creamy.*
- *Add 1 tsp. vanilla after mixture boils.*
- *Serve over ice cream, warm or refrigerated for future use.*

Adjustments:
If one prefers a more Bitter-Sweet Chocolate – Chocolate, substitute 8 oz. unsweetened chocolate for 8 oz. of semi-sweet and increase the half and half to 3½ cups.

Cranberry Sauce

Thanksgiving turkeys were always accompanied by cranberry sauce. This was originally Mom's specialty and every year the big mystery was whether the sauce would hold its shape when removed from the aluminum mold. We seem to remember that the odds were about thirty-seventy against. In more recent years Michael took over with moderate success. Michael's theory is that success or failure in this regard had nothing to do with the recipe. Michael insists that the condition of the cranberries involved will dictate whether the sauce holds its shape. Fresher or perhaps more expensive cranberries may (or may not) increase the chance of holding the mold. It is difficult to tell because one doesn't know whether he/she is getting fresh cranberries. Michael bases his opinion on the recipe which is for a sauce, and while Mom experimented with gelatin, she did, on occasion succeed with the basic recipe. While the original recipe is listed below, the Royal Couple, has perfected and included an alternative recipe that is undoubtedly a sauce, eliminating the requirement for a perfectly formed mold.

Cranberries (Mom/Michael)

The Ingredients:
- cranberries, sugar, water

The Recipe:
- Bring 1 cup water and 1 cup sugar to the boil in a medium sauce pan making sure that the sugar is fully dissolved.
- Add 1 12 oz. package of cranberries and return to boil.
- Reduce heat to low boil and cook for 10 minutes, stirring occasionally.
- Remove from heat and place in a covered serving dish or mold and allow to cool.
- Once cool, refrigerate.

Adjustments:
To have any chance of the cranberries holding a mold shape follow the instructions carefully. Also use high-end cranberries (Ocean Spray). If you are making more cranberries than the recipe calls

for, make two separate batches rather than doubling up the recipe.

Michael – perfection   Mom - perfection

Cranberries (Robert and Pamela)

The Ingredients:
- *fresh cranberries, sugar, Amaretto, orange, almonds*

The Recipe:
- *Mix 2/3 cup sugar, 2/3 cup water, 1/3 cup Amaretto in a pot and bring to boil.*
- *Add 12 oz. fresh cranberries and return to boil.*
- *Reduce heat and boil gently for 8-10 minutes stirring often.*
- *Remove from heat, add juice from one orange and 1 tbsp. orange zest.*

- *Allow to cool, refrigerate and served chilled.*

Adjustments:
While this recipe calls for toasted almonds to be added before serving, that is an option. After preparation, this concoction may be frozen with chunks cut off and defrosted for later use.

Tomato Relish

This recipe arrives courtesy of Pat who holds the original with Nanna's handwritten notes. She apparently acquired it from Mrs. John J. Boland Sr. In this day of purchasing relish of all varieties off the shelf in the grocery stores, this recipe reminds us of a time when it was a bit more complicated. Perhaps we should all have a go at recreating this recipe.

The Ingredients:
- *green tomatoes, white onions, cider vinegar, salt, dried mustard, pepper, allspice, clove, sugar*

The Recipe:
- *Mix in a large pot 2 gal. sliced green tomatoes, 12 good sized white onions sliced, 2 qts. cider vinegar, 2 tbsp. salt, 2 tbsp. dried mustard, 2 tbsp. black pepper, 1 tbsp. ground allspice, 1 tbsp. ground clove, 2 qts. sugar.*
- *Bring to boil and then simmer slowly, stirring occasionally for 4-5 hours or until the tomatoes and onions are tender.*
- *Seal in jars while relish is still hot.*

HAPPY HOUR

Although the younger generation might think the "It's five o'clock somewhere" is a recent expression...Aunt Sheila, wink...wink..., actually, Happy Hour in the Connolly Family has been a tradition for at least a couple generations as you can clearly see from a picture taken nearly 70 years ago. Not every day mind you, but certainly on weekends and other special occasions. Happy Hours consisted of an adult beverage...for adults... and "something to keep me from getting silly," as Grammy was fond of saying. In this chapter we will explore Happy Hour including both the adult beverages and the hors d'oeuvres. Perhaps it is not surprising that this is the longest chapter in our exploration of Connolly Family recipes.

·Gram and Nanna – Were the ladies set up?
1949, on the occasion of Pat's Baptism

115

Old Fashioned

What better place to start than with the official recipe for an Old Fashioned. This was the go-to drink on cold winter evenings. The recipe was perfected and passed on by Dad. Grammy loved her Old Fashioned and allowed her grandchildren to finish the fruit garnishments…although she did draw the line at licking the alcohol off and redipping…Robert. Pamela claims that a nice Old Fashioned will send a cold or sore throat packing so it has moved to Dublin and beyond. A word of warning…if Pat happens to be giving haircuts to her brothers at about the same time, you want to be first in line for the chop before things become too loose. When Uncle Pat died in Escondido, his children and extended family toasted his life with in-excess-of one and a half gallons of Old Fashioneds. Some mathematics was applied to determine, for example, how many drops of bitters were in a half-cup. We are pleased to report that Pat, Mary, Billy and Robert were in attendance but did not significantly participate in this debauchery. Although Robert is the current custodian of the official silver shot measure, which will undoubtedly be bequeathed to some very lucky niece/nephew, the proportions listed below are based on that measure.

The Ingredients:
- *bourbon/whiskey, bitters, sugar, maraschino cherries, lemon, orange, candied ginger*

The Recipe:
- *Mix in cocktail shaker, 2 oz. of Imperial blended whiskey, 7 drops Angostura bitters, 1 heaping tsp. sugar, 1 "heaping tsp. water" – said Dad.*

- *Shake with a couple ice cubes and ensure sugar is dissolved.*
- *Garnish glass with a slice of orange and lemon, a maraschino cherry and a small lump of candied ginger.*
- *Serve over ice.*

Adjustments:

A splash of the cherry juice can add that bit of sweetness some people like. Imperial whiskey is not universally available...and certainly not in Ireland. Remarkably, using Jameson or any fine Irish whiskey makes the drink incredibly smooth. In a pinch, other whiskeys and or bourbons...even Canadian or Scotch- for those who like Scotch- are not completely unpalatable.

Uncle John, Dad, Uncle Pat, Gramp (Connolly) -
celebrating after Pat's baptism

Anchovy Spread

This recipe dates back a couple of generations to either Nanna or, perhaps, Aunt Mary Connolly O'Donovan…that would be Dad's sister. It was certainly the ideal way to stop Grammy from getting silly. When our generation was growing up, we were very lucky to get even one cracker because, were we to descend on the appetizer…as can currently be the case with the next generation… there would not be enough left to stop any silliness at all. However, on a rare occasion, small broken pieces of Melba toast were dipped into the anchovy oil, or oyster/sardine oil if they were the appetizer, and passed out to those lurking about. This was the case with virtually all appetizers but all was not lost… later on we will discuss appetizers for the masses.

The Ingredients:
- *anchovies, garlic clove, cream cheese, Melba toast*

The Recipe:
- *Mash together 1 can of anchovies, drained of oil, and chopped up, 1 garlic clove (not bulb) squeezed through a press, 1 8 oz. package of regular Philadelphia cream cheese.*
- *Spread over Melba toast.*

Adjustments:
If this hors d'oeuvre is made in advance, the Melba toast can become soggy so serve as you go. Although purists (Michael) might insist on using regular/full fat cream cheese others, more interested in maintaining our girlish figures, find that lower fat cream cheese is also enjoyable. Philadelphia even manufactures a low fat garlic

and herb cream cheese that is very nice and eliminates the need for the garlic clove which can overpower the spread. Finally, if Melba toast is not available, experiment with other types of crackers.

Katy and Robert - early Old Fashioned lessons

Whiskey Sour

It would appear in more recent times that Whiskey Sour has surpassed the Old Fashioned at special cold weather holidays like Thanksgiving and Christmas. Perhaps that is because it is easier to make in volume, which has become necessary as the number of family members who are entitled to enjoy adult beverages has expanded exponentially. We have Jack to thank for this...the recipe not the exponential expansion.

The Ingredients:
- *bourbon/blended whiskey, frozen lemonade, orange, lemon, maraschino cherries*

The Recipe:
- *Mix well in a large pitcher, 1 can frozen lemonade, 1 can water, 1 can Imperial/ Canadian Club/blended whiskey.*
- *Serve over ice and garnish with an orange slice and a cherry.*

Adjustments:
Unfortunately, frozen lemonade is not available in Ireland and that seems to be the vital ingredient; so enjoy your whiskey sours in the United States. Of course, you can experiment with other types of whiskey, e.g. Irish, for a smoother taste.

Jack - brewing multiple Whiskey Sours

Clam Dip

This remarkable concoction has been a long-standing crowd pleaser during Connolly Happy Hours. Its origins may be lost in the mists of time but we will attribute it to Mom because she was the expert. In Fort Wayne, this dip was served with locally manufactured Seyfert's Potato Chips, which are not universally available. As was the case with most appetizers, enjoyment of this treat was restricted to the adults. If we were lucky, we might get one chip with a bit of dip. However, an alternative was sometimes provided. The remnants of an old, and occasionally stale, bag of Seyfert's was available and passed down to the unwashed masses. Mary would then make her favorite dip, cottage cheese and horseradish, or perhaps, sour cream and dried French's onion soup. We would dig in....Yummm.

The Ingredients:
- cream cheese, Coleman's dried mustard, Miracle Whip, Tabasco, Worcestershire sauce, canned clams, potato chips

The Recipe:
- *Mix until smooth: 1 8 oz. package Philadelphia cream cheese, 1 heaping tbsp. Miracle Whip, 1 tsp. Coleman's dried mustard, a couple dashes of Tabasco sauce and a couple dashes of Worcestershire sauce.*
- *Open 1 can minced/chopped clams.*
- *Pour some clam juice into cream cheese mix to achieve desired dip consistency.*
- *Drain off the clams and add clams to the dip and stir.*

- *Fold in freshly chopped chives to finish the dip.*
- *Serve with potato chips.*

Adjustments:
This dip is excellent with a wide range of potato chips so don't hesitate to experiment. As is the case with Anchovy Spread, there are those in our family who are horrified at talk of using anything but regular/full fat Philadelphia cream cheese...others not so much. Philadelphia makes a low fat cheese with chives that works well particularly when the garden isn't producing. Michael has adjusted by using two cans of clams so if you love clams.... Finally, where Miracle Whip is not available, a mayonnaise based salad spread will also work.

Beer

In deference to some of the younger generation who have not yet discovered more civilized cocktails, we present this staple. We will give Kevin credit for passing on beer to the next generation although we are not sure he has embraced the wide range of craft products the younger ones seem to enjoy. Katy has generously shared her favorites which, she assures us, should be available for years to come. Specifically, during the Winter, a higher alcohol beer should keep you warm; so, Bell's Expedition Stout is just the thing. Welcoming the warmer Spring weather is a perfect opportunity to enjoy Flying Dog Hefeweizen. An ideal sipping beer for those Summer cookouts would certainly be Lagunitas Day Time IPA. While in the Autumn, with a nip in the air, Great Lakes Eliot Ness Amber Lager is ideal for watching a football game.

The Ingredients:
- *beer of choice*

The Recipe;
- *Place bottles/cans of selected beer in the fridge.*
- *Cool to 30 to 34 F.*
- *Remove cap/tab and enjoy.*

Adjustments:
It is permissible to pour the contents into a glass before drinking. There are two schools of thought on this procedure, down the side to minimize foam, or down the middle to minimize gas. To each his/her own. If it is particularly hot, beer over ice cut with seven-up or lemonade (a Shandy) can be particularly refreshing.

Richard, Lauren, and Michael – Christmas cheers

Artichoke Dip

This dip is another tasty and simple treat which has become a staple on both sides of the Atlantic. The recipe's Connolly roots originate with Joan. Because it is sinfully rich and, depending on how much you consume, it may not be necessary to move on to dinner.

The Ingredients:
- *artichoke hearts, mayonnaise, fresh parmesan cheese, garlic powder*

The Recipe:
- *Drain one large can of artichoke hearts.*
- *Mix the chopped artichoke hearts, 1 cup mayonnaise, 1 cup grated fresh parmesan cheese.*
- *Add dash of garlic powder to taste.*
- *Bake in deep dish at 350° F. for 20 minutes.*
- *Serve on crackers.*

Adjustments:
Although this is a hearty snack in its own right, some people have added chives, and/or bacon bits. For a bit of color, a sprinkling of paprika adds a nice touch. This appetizer can be served on a wide range of crackers including the most basic, saltines. It should be allowed to cool just a bit as it is quite hot and bubbly out of the oven.

Martini

Like other cocktails, the martini has undergone a significant evolution from the days it was served in prohibition era speakeasies. For example, you would seldom get a dash of orange bitters these days but that was included in early recipes.

As can be seen in the adjustments, use of vermouth has also changed. This recipe is included because during the warmer months, Dad would often mix a Martini, as opposed to an Old Fashioned, if he was serving cocktails. Adopting the mantra of his father, the original Robert Emmet, Dad maintained a martini was the perfect aperitif for a good steak. Dad also informed us that his father used to enjoy a martini with ½ dozen blue point oysters in New York's Grand Central Train Station's Oyster Bar before lunch... those were the days! In memory of his namesake, the current Robert Emmet always makes the same order at the same location whenever he is in New York City. For those concerned about youthful figures, vodka has no sugar and fewer calories/carbohydrates than virtually any other adult beverage.

The Ingredients:
- *gin/vodka, vermouth, olives*

The Recipe:
- *Mix in cocktail shaker 2 ounces of gin and a splash of dry vermouth.*
- *Either pour over ice or shake with ice and strain pouring into a martini glass.*
- *Garnish with an olive.*

Adjustments:
The primary adjustment that has developed over the years is substituting vodka for gin. Some people do not appreciate the distinctive taste of juniper berries attributed to gin so vodka has become the alternative. The original Martini recipe called for two thirds gin/vodka and one third vermouth. However, the proportion of vermouth decreased to a splash and then to rinsing the glass with vermouth before dumping it out. The current practice is to just wave the vermouth bottle over the glass without adding any at all...known

as gin/vodka on ice/the rocks. Olives are still permitted. Another variation is to add a twist of lemon instead of an olive. There are also now a wide range of olives from stuffed with pimentos to blue cheese to anchovies. There are also those who like a dirty martini which includes a splash of olive juice. A couple words of warning on ordering Martinis...if you want gin/vodka on the rocks order that or you will be charged for a cocktail. Finally, if you order a Martini in Ireland, you will get dry vermouth on the rocks; so either order an American Martini or gin/vodka on ice. By way of warning, the cheaper the gin/vodka the worse the hangover. Modern bars and liquor stores stock a selection of flavored vodkas including orange, lemon, blackberry, etc. etc. So, if one is into such varieties, a wide range of new "martinis" is on offer.

Mom, Kitty, Hilda, John - toasting the Florida sunset

Parmesan Toast

This recipe originates with Cath and although it is very simple to make, few people seem to be able to identify its ingredients. Having travelled across the ocean it has become a popular favorite with Pamela's aged mother and aunt who appreciate its gentle taste.

The Ingredients:
- *dried onions, mayonnaise, French bread, fresh parmesan*

The Recipe:
- *Soak 2 tsp. dried onions in boiling water for 10 minutes to reconstitute the onions; then drain off the water.*
- *Stir in ½ cup mayonnaise, ¼ cup grated fresh parmesan cheese.*
- *Slice a loaf of French bread into 1 inch angled slices.*
- *Toast one side of bread in broiler.*
- *Spread concoction on uncooked side.*
- *Place on oven rack and bake for 10 minutes at 350° F. or until cheese starts to brown.*

Adjustments:
For a bit more flavor, consider adding additional reconstituted onions or perhaps a bit of garlic powder. Chives and/or bacon bits can be added while a sprinkling of paprika over the top gives a nice bit of color.

Richard, Cath, Katy, Lauren, Sheila -
Flossmoor...bring on the appetizers

Manhattan

Many adult beverage cocktails which survive from the 50s and before are becoming increasingly rare, replaced by fufu drinks and other sweet concoctions which require far less time to acquire "the taste for." We include the Manhattan, not only because it was an alternative to the Old Fashioned, but because it was the drink of choice for Fr. Phillip Neenan. Fr. Neenan became acquainted with our family when he ran the youth club at St. Gabriel's Church on the south side of Chicago in the late 1930s and early 40s. Mom and her best friend Cele Wilhelm (who, coincidently was Fr. Neenan's cousin) were regular participants. (One might note the engraving on the bowling trophy awarded to a "grown-up" the day after Christmas – "Fr. Neenan Tournament 1942 Eileen Murphy.") Subsequently, Fr. Neenan presided at Mom's wedding, and each of the family's weddings until he died in 1995. In 1986, after he retired, Mom

128

and Cele travelled with him to Rome and had a private audience with Pope (St.) John Paul II, on the occasion of Father's 50th anniversary of ordination. Fr. Neenan was fond of saying that he never bought green bananas. He died of a heart attack at age 84 immediately after tipping a bus driver in Tahiti... which leads us to Fr. Neenan's drink of choice - Manhattans. In fact, when he was waked at his parish, among the mementos neatly laid out at the back of the church, were his biretta, breviary, chalice and a Manhattan. At the brunch following the Mass, Manhattans were served in his memory. Obviously, when visiting Fort Wayne, we served this fine cocktail and Father would say, Robert served the best he'd ever had....take that with a grain of salt as we are sure, in his kindness, he said that to anyone who served him a Manhattan.

The Ingredients:
- *bourbon/blended whiskey, bitters, sweet vermouth, maraschino cherry*

The Recipe;
- *Mix in a cocktail shaker, 4 ounces Imperial or other blended whiskey, 2 ounce sweet (Italian) vermouth, 1 dash Angostura bitters.*
- *Serve over ice and garnish with a maraschino cherry.*

Adjustments:
As is the case with many traditional cocktails, the Manhattan has evolved over the years. A recipe from the 1930s, for example, called for ½ rye whiskey, ½ sweet vermouth and a dash of bitters. Today, much like a Martini, tastes change. Rye is rare so bourbon has taken its place... as with the case of the Old Fashioned, Irish whiskey makes for a smooth alternative. Again, like the Martini, some people prefer only a splash, or even less, of

129

vermouth and some modern recipes eliminate bitters altogether. Finally, some people prefer their Manhattan shaken with ice and served neat, in a martini glass, with a cherry, of course.

Marion, Mom, Cele and Fr. Neenan – toasting an adventure

Shrimp Dip

Shrimp Dip was another dip at 4305, Ridge Valley and the various places in which we have settled. As was the case with other appetizers, we seldom had a shot at more than one chip, but we have since more than made up for our suffering. Once again, this dip was served with Seyfert's Potato Chips but there are now many other brands, including popular specialist Irish brands like O'Donnell's and Connolly's which are very nice.

The Ingredients:
- *chili sauce, lemon juice, salt, pepper, horseradish, Tabasco, sour cream, shrimp, potato chips*

The Recipe:

- *Mix in a dip bowl, ¼ cup chili sauce, 2 tsp. lemon juice, ½ tsp. salt, 1/8 tsp. pepper, 1 tsp. horseradish, 1 dash Tabasco.*
- *Fold in 1 cup sour cream.*
- *Add 2/3 cup of shrimp chopped into bits.*
- *Serve chilled with potato chips.*

Adjustments

Where canned shrimp is available, one 4½ oz. can replace the fresh/frozen shrimp. Some people prefer a bit more horseradish to give more kick. Typically, use straight horseradish, where available as opposed to creamed. Where American chili sauce is not available (Ireland) a generic tomato based hamburger relish will also work. Of course, there is nothing wrong with several extra shrimps.

Mike and Mary - hosts with the most

Apple Dip

For a bit sweeter appetizer, Joan has provided this recipe courtesy of her sister-in-law, Sue Nieman. While more savory (salty or non-sweet) treats work well with more traditional cocktails this hors d'oeuvre will complement wines, and fufu drinks, preferably with an umbrella....or perhaps Irish Cream. (recipe below)

The Ingredients:
- *cream cheese, brown sugar, white sugar, vanilla, salted peanuts, apples, lemon juice*

The Recipe:
- *Mix into a dipping bowl 1 softened 8 oz. package Philadelphia cream cheese, ¾ cup brown sugar, ¼ cup white sugar, 1 tbsp. vanilla and ½ cup finely crushed salted peanuts.*
- *Slice apples into crescents and dip in lemon juice to prevent the apples from browning.*
- *Serve using apples to dip into concoction.*

Sam, Lauren, Mitch, Michael, Máire, Katy -
plenty of cheers

Pineapple Cheese Spread

This is another sweeter appetizer originating in Joan's kitchen, or perhaps from the O'Connors, but certainly compliments a pre-dinner glass, or two, of wine.

The Ingredients:
- *cream cheese, pecans, crushed pineapple, green peppers, onion, seasoned salt, bread rounds*

The Recipe:
- *Beat 1 softened 8 oz. package Philadelphia cream cheese until fluffy.*
- *Stir in 1 cup chopped pecans, 1 8½ oz. can crushed pineapple, well drained, ¼ cup chopped green peppers, 2 tbsp. chopped onion, ½ tbsp. seasoned salt.*
- *Serve on bread rounds or crackers.*

Fionn – even Finny loved Irish Cream

Irish Cream

This recipe originates with Cath and provides an inexpensive substitute for Bailey's Irish Cream and a wide variety of similar products, which were a bit dear before Dublin Duty Free became a more permanent fixture.

The Ingredients:
- *Eagle Brand condensed milk, Coffee Rich creamer, Hershey's chocolate sauce, coconut extract, bourbon*

The Recipe:
- *Mix 1 can Eagle Brand condensed milk, 10 oz. Coffee Rich creamer, 3 tsp. Hershey's chocolate sauce, ½ tsp. coconut extract, 1½ cup bourbon.*
- *Chill and serve over ice.*

Adjustments:
As with many, whiskey based drinks, a variety of bourbons/blended whiskeys are acceptable. Since the original Bailey's actually uses Irish whiskey that would be the preference. The artificial creamer in this recipe is intended to allow the finished product to spend some time in the refrigerator without going off, but if immediate consumption is anticipated, real cream is preferred. Some people like a more chocolate taste, so adding a bit more chocolate sauce is permitted.

Robert and Sheila – Happy Hour in Ireland

Tortilla Pinwheels

Moving toward more ethnic options, Joan presents her Mexican specialty.   Such an esoteric dish would have been unheard of at 4305 where the only thing remotely Hispanic was Fritos Corn Chips. This treat would go well with a Margarita or a bottle of Corona.

The Ingredients:
- *cream cheese, sour cream, picante sauce, green chilies, cheddar, garlic powder, seasoned salt, flour tortillas*

The Recipe:
- *Blend 1 8 oz. package regular Philadelphia cream cheese, 1 cup sour cream, 3 tbsp. medium heat picante sauce, 1 4 oz. bottle/can of green chilies chopped, 1 cup*

shredded cheddar, dash garlic powder,
dash of seasoned salt.
- *Spread over 5 ten inch flour tortillas.*
- *Roll up tortillas and wrap in cling film/plastic wrap; chill overnight.*
- *Serve in ½ inch slices.*

Margarita

Be careful with these because they are sweet and easy to drink or you might get wasted away. Perhaps some pinwheels or nachos will stop you from getting silly. Our examination of Margaritas would not be complete without telling the tale of enjoying this concoction in Las Vegas. Sheila, Robert, Pamela and Cait were wandering the strip when they came across Jimmy Buffett's Margaritaville and it only seemed right to stop in for a drink at the sidewalk bar and enjoy a bit of people watching. The bartender requested identification from Pamela and Cait to ensure they were of age. Sheila asked whether the barman needed to see her ID as well. His response, "Just those two...I don't care what you do." Sheila was mortified.... 'The neck' on him.

The Ingredients:
- *tequila, lime juice, triple sec*

The Recipe:
- *Blend one part triple sec, two parts lime juice, three parts tequila.*
- *Shake well garnish with lime and serve over ice.*

Adjustments:
   Nearly every 'expert' has their own way of creating this popular drink. The obvious adjustments are to either serve over ice or using a blender serve as a frozen concoction to help you hang on.

Also…with or without salt on the rim, a rub with a lime ensures the salt sticks. Some people prefer to use a margarita mix which is certainly acceptable but the directions on the back might be slightly different. Another variation uses cointreau instead of triple sec and there are those who eliminate the liqueur completely. Others, including our good friend and 'sista from a different mista,' Linda Maier, maintain that only tequila with blue agave will do.

Mary and Ewelina - cheers

Nachos

By the time party central moved to Ridge Valley, Nachos had begun to make a regular appearance at happy hour. While there are many variations, the initial offering included microwaving a lump of processed cheese, mixing in salsa and dipping using tortilla chips. This gave way to a bit more civilized confection which is described below.

The Ingredients:
- *tortilla chips, salsa, cheddar cheese*

The Recipe:
- *Spread tortilla chips on a sheet of aluminum foil.*
- *Drizzle salsa, (mild/medium) and spread shredded white cheddar cheese over the chips.*
- *Cook under broiler until the cheese is fully melted.*

Adjustments:
This recipe would be the most basic of all possibilities, apart from also eliminating the salsa. The variety of adjustments is hindered only by the imagination of the chef. Among the most popular would include spreading browned ground beef/cooked chicken before drizzling the salsa (or perhaps barbecue sauce) Adding additional ingredients like chopped tomatoes, jalapeño peppers or chopped onions is also popular. The cheese does not have to be cheddar as any shredded cheese will do and using a spicier salsa is also permitted. After removing from the broiler, many people top up with sour cream, guacamole or even lettuce. Experiment and enjoy.

Sunny Southwest Dip

Another recipe with origins in Mexican cuisine comes courtesy of Joan. We suspect that with Joan there is a certain comfort in not having to worry about one's girlish figure including freedom to not feel guilty about consuming calorie rich specialties. When the Royal Couple was first married, himself was keen to demonstrate his range of specialties during a daily happy hour. Several pounds later this practice was significantly curtailed but it is always nice...once in a while. Because it is always necessary to support those who support us, always use Tabasco as your hot sauce. Tabasco, invented in 1868 by a Donegal man Henry McIlheny, has been brewed since then in New Iberia, Louisiana by the McIlheny Family. Since the family died out, profits from Tabasco support the Glenveagh National Park in Donegal.

The Ingredients:
- *frozen corn, butter, red peppers, black beans, Colby jack cheese, cumin, mayonnaise, Tabasco, tortilla chips*

The Recipe:
- *Mix into frying pan 1 bag frozen corn, ½ stick butter, ½ cup chopped red peppers, ½ cup black beans.*
- *Sauté for 10-15 minutes.*
- *Mix in large bowl: 1½ cup shredded Colby jack, 2-3 tsp. cumin, 1 cup mayonnaise, dash Tabasco.*
- *Combine mixtures and pour into shallow pan.*
- *Bake at 350° F. for 10 minutes.*
- *Serve with tortilla chips or crackers.*

Adjustments:
Some people prefer a bit more (or less) heat achieved with more Tabasco or perhaps jalapeños. Yellow or orange peppers would add a bit more color. Oher types of cheese could be interesting...depending on one's taste.

Sangria

Sangria is not something that would have been served at 4305, Ridge Valley or Fort Wayne in general, but we have included it because the Royal Couple dictates. Actually, it is a refreshing change to summer dining, particularly when serving Hispanic based recipes like the paella Julie has presented in the Dinner section. This drink recipe originates in San Pedro in the south of Spain, where Pamela and Robert dined at a particularly nice restaurant enjoying sangria and paella. Returning a few days later, they were recognized as return customers and the Sangria packed a bit more punch. The establishment was kind enough to provide this recipe which, for special customers, contains the special ingredient, cognac.

The Ingredients:
- *lemons, limes, oranges, strawberries, sugar, dry red wine, cognac, club soda*

The Recipe:
- *Combine in a large pitcher ½ thinly sliced lime, ½ thinly sliced lemon, ½ thinly sliced orange, 6-8 strawberries, ½ cup sugar, 1 750 ml. bottle of dry red wine, ¼ cup cognac, 2 cups club soda.*
- *Mash the fruit in pitcher, dissolve the sugar and chill.*
- *Serve over ice.*

 Adjustments:
 Sangria is essentially a wine and fruit combination so any fruit is acceptable including cherries, other berries, pineapple, etc. Pamela is allergic to

strawberries, she excludes them. For authenticity, a Spanish rioja is particularly nice.

Guacamole Dip

Continuing with the theme of Southwest/Hispanic specialties, this recipe is courtesy of Pamela who acquired it from her cousins in Chicago. It is a healthy option...more or less.

The Ingredients:
- *avocados lemon juice, green chilies, shallot, olive oil, salt, Tabasco, tortilla chips*

The Recipe:
- *Cut two ripe avocados in half, remove stones and mash well on a plate then move to a bowl.*
- *Add 1 tbsp. lemon juice, 1 small diced clove of garlic, 1 small finely chopped and seeded green chili, 1 finely chopped shallot and mix well.*
- *Stir in 1 tbsp. olive oil, dash of salt and dash of Tabasco sauce, and chill dip before serving.*
- *Serve with tortilla chips.*

Adjustments:
Some people use a press to add the garlic while others prefer to eliminate the garlic altogether. Finely sliced green onions can replace the shallots.

141

Colin, Michael, Luke, Conor, Kevin - shrimp disappearing fast

Sʜʀɪᴍᴘ Cocᴋᴛᴀɪʟ

At Cath's house, a least when there wasn't a gang of young ones around, Happy Hour would include a wedge of the Danish blue cheese she particularly liked and Shrimp Cocktail. One can easily purchase cooked shrimp or a wheel of shrimp with cocktail sauce. However, such shrimp can be a bit mushy. Cath's were different – always firm and crispy. She cleaned and cooked them herself. This is the recipe she used, subsequently adopted by Robert and others who prefer Cath-style shrimp.

The Ingredients:
- *shrimp, chili sauce, horseradish, salt, saltine crackers*

The Recipe:
For the Sauce:

- *In a small bowl, mix chili sauce (amount depends on number of shrimp) and horseradish sauce to taste.*

For the Shrimp:
- *Place raw, shelled and deveined shrimp with a pinch of salt into boiling water and cook until the shrimp turns red/white and the tail curls.*
- *Pour shrimp into a colander and spray with cold water until all heat has been eliminated and the shrimp is cold.*
- *Dry shrimp and refrigerated on paper towel for a minimum of two hours until ready to serve.*

Adjustments:

This recipe works well with either fresh or frozen raw shrimp. When using frozen shrimp the time to remove and spray the shrimp is generally just before the water returns to the boil. Fresh shrimp will cook more quickly. Another adjustment is to boil the shrimp in a shrimp boil mixture which is available at many stores or, invent your own with a bit of cayenne pepper, garlic powder, oregano, all-spice or whatever looks good on your spice rack. It will be washed off, of course, when you spray the shrimp to abruptly stop the cooking but traces of the flavors will remain. When making the cocktail sauce, the pinker the sauce, the hotter it becomes but one can always add of bit of one ingredient or the other until it is perfect.

Mint Julep

This beverage was trotted out on extremely rare occasions in the summer time, usually in June around Dad's birthday, when

Cath and Nanna, who particularly enjoyed her mint julep, would visit. It was a complex process which included breaking out the ice crusher with the green plastic bottom that attached to the counter as well as putting aluminum 'glasses' (which it seems were only used for Mint Juleps) into the freezer. Another special item employed was a stretchy cloth sleeve which kept one's hands from freezing on the aluminum glass.

The Ingredients:
- *bourbon/blended whiskey, mint, powdered sugar*

The Recipe:
- *Crush (also known as muddling) 4-5 mint leaves, 1 tsp. powdered sugar and 2 tsp. water. This entails mashing the concoction with the round or flat handle of a wooden spoon or a muddler, until the flavor of the mint is fully released.*
- *Fill glass with crushed ice.*
- *Mix muddled mint with 2½ oz. of Imperial and shake in cocktail shaker with a couple cubes of ice.*
- *Pour over crushed ice into 'glasses.'*
- *Garnish with a couple of mint leaves and serve with a straw.*

Adjustments:
In the likely event that aluminum glasses are not available, although perhaps someone has inherited them, ordinary glasses are also permitted. The important ingredient is ice. The glasses should be well-chilled, filled with crushed ice, and the concoction also chilled before serving. Of course, this recipe can be mixed in a pitcher proportionally increasing the ingredients.

Dad at the grill – Mom and Nana at Mint Juleps

Crab Spread

This is another Happy Hour appetizer that kept Connollys from getting silly at Ridge Valley Drive. The recipe is quite basic with any number of variations, some of which eliminate crab completely. Mom presented this treat on the aluminum pizza trays, but a plate works equally well.

The Ingredients:
- *cream cheese, chili sauce, horseradish, canned crab, Wheat Thins/Triscuits*

The Recipe:
- *Spread 1 8 oz. package Philadelphia cream cheese evenly on the surface of a tray or plate.*

- *Spread a cocktail sauce (see condiments), essentially chili sauce and horseradish, evenly over the cream cheese.*
- *Sprinkle 1 can of crumbled crab meat over the top.*
- *Serve with Wheat Thins or Triscuits.*

Adjustments:
Additional crab meat is certainly permitted and some people have found that several sticks of pseudo crab chopped add a bit of bulk when combined with real crab. On occasion, this hors d'oeuvre was altered completely as salsa replaced the cocktail sauce and other Mexican toppings e.g. ground beef and shredded cheese completed the dip. It is served with tortilla chips.

Pina Colada

On occasion Robert would break out the blender and create a wide range of cocktails. By replacing the alcoholic ingredients with 7-Up or some other juice, it was possible to create alcohol free drinks to be enjoyed by those under the legal drinking age. Rather than exploring the range we will include a Pina Colada and discuss variations in the adjustment.

The Ingredients:
- *rum, coconut milk, crushed pineapple, sliced pineapple*

The Recipe:
- *Mix 4 oz. rum, 6 tbsp. condensed coconut milk and a healthy splash of pineapple juice in blender.*
- *Add ½ cup of crushed pineapple and ice.*

- *Blend until ice is crushed and drink gains a smooth consistency.*
- *Serve in a tall glass garnished with sliced pineapple, a maraschino, a straw and, if available, an umbrella.*

Adjustments:

In creating any of these umbrella drinks the key is to use condensed milk or condensed coconut milk to provide a thick and smooth consistency and, obviously, plenty of calories. After that, it is just a matter of deciding what milk, what fruit and what alcohol goes together. For example, to make Mary's favorite Strawberry Daiquiri, vodka, condensed milk and strawberries (out of season, frozen fruit works well because there is plenty of juice) blended with ice until smooth creates a nice consistency. There are now a wide range of mixes which come in bottles, requiring only alcohol, ice and blending, and these would be an easy shortcut. As mentioned above, by replacing the alcohol with orange, pineapple or any berry juice, young ones can enjoy a good sugar boost.

Robert – breaking out the blender

Yogurt and Feta Dip

As one might suspect, Katy has offered this recipe in the interest of a more healthy Happy Hour which, some would say, defeats the whole purpose of "eating before you eat!" and drinking a range of sugared-up drinks or full calorie beers. Needless to say, it has become a welcome alternative on the Christmas Day appetizer table at the McManus house or wherever she is responsible for a dip. Well done, Katy, for keeping us on the straight and narrow.

The Ingredients:
- *Greek yogurt, feta cheese, sundried tomatoes, Kalamata olives, oregano, dill, lemon juice, pepper, cucumbers*

The Recipe:
- *Combine 3 tbsp. plain Greek yogurt, 6 oz. crumbled feta cheese and mash together with a fork.*
- *Add 3 tbsp. sliced sundried tomatoes, 8-12 pitted Kalamata olives chopped, 1 tbsp. dill or oregano (chopped), 2 tsp. lemon juice, dash of pepper to taste.*
- *Chill and serve with thinly sliced cucumbers.*

Adjustments:
The recipe can be doubled or trebled to accommodate the number of guests. If you want to be very indulgent you can serve this dip on crackers or bread rounds...Katy always goes full fat - just in moderation. Of course, she is definitely on board with whole wheat.

Dandelion Wine

Here is a recipe that few of us would have expected to see but, fortunately, Pat came across it in her travels. It is, perhaps, one of the oldest recipes in our collection and most certainly a family tradition. Apparently, Nanna received it from an 'unknown friend' who thought a wee nip might just be the thing that her sister, our Grand Aunt Ethel Kane might need to "set her up." Who are we to argue with such logic? Perhaps a word about Aunt Ethel would be in order. Nanna's sister was regarded as the sickly one who apparently contracted a strain of tuberculosis as a young woman. With the support of Nanna's husband, the original Robert Emmet, Ethel retired to the Adirondack Mountains to die. Ultimately, she did die... sixty years later... but she seldom, if ever ventured out of the mountains. John and Robert camped on her front lawn during a trip east. She was delightful company, proudly cooking the one dish she was familiar with, a soft boiled egg. The boys spent an evening with her going through her photo albums including scenes from the beach at Fire Island. That would have been during the roaring twenties and Aunt Ethel was undoubtedly a very beautiful flapper. Robert specifically recalls one picture of Aunt Ethel on the beach. Although the bathing outfit reached down to her knees, its material was quite the opposite of heavy wool, leaving little to the imagination. Years later, he went looking through pictures in Cath's attic and although Aunt Ethel's album was located, several pictures, including the Sports Illustrated Cover Model had been removed leaving black holes. We digress... Pat also offers this recipe to remember inadequately paid young dandelion pickers. We shall add a word for similarly inadequately paid mulberry pickers when their brothers were brewing mulberry wine. As the story goes, the boys got their comeuppance when late one night several bottle of fermenting brew exploded in their basement bedroom, showering the place with mulberry wine.

The Ingredients:
- dandelion flowers, oranges, lemons, sugar

The Recipe:
- Mix 1 gal. dandelion flowers, (yellow part only.. botanically known as corolla... lesson courtesy of unknown friend..) 1 gal. water, peels of 3 orange and 3 lemons..
- Bring concoction to boil and simmer for 15 minutes.
- Strain through a cheese cloth and add 3 lbs. sugar and juice from the oranges and lemons.
- Pour into bottles or jugs and set out in the sun allowing to ferment.
- When the fermentation action ceases, cork and put away for future consumption.

Adjustments:
Having never actually tried this recipe, it would be inappropriate to suggest any adjustments, however from experience with mulberry wine, allowing the fermentation process to end, before corking, is an excellent ideal because that process can blow the cork off any bottle. That is the reason champagne corks are wired on... fermentation continues in the bottle.

Anne and Sheila – wine goes with everything

Cheese Ball

Being a big fan of blue cheese this recipe was one of Dad's favorites. Mom obliged though not a fan. As with other appetizers the rest of the family might have had a passing sniff at this treat, but not much else.

The Ingredients:
- *cream cheese, cheddar cheese, blue cheese, onion, Worcestershire sauce, milk, pecan, parsley, crackers*

The Recipe:
- *Blend (in blender) 2-3 oz. cream cheese, ¼ cup grated cheddar, 3 oz. blue cheese, 1*

finely chopped small onion wedge, 1 tsp. Worcestershire Sauce, ¼ cup milk.
- *Form cheese mix into a ball.*
- *Mix ½ cup chopped pecans, 6 sprigs chopped parsley.*
- *Roll cheese ball on pecans/parsley.*
- *Serve on crackers.*

Curry Dip

Lest anyone believe that Katy is the only healthy option specialist, Pat has frequently produced this dip along with an extremely artistically designed collection of vegetables. One hardly wants to remove a bit of broccoli from the arrangement but guilt, for having indulged in far too many cream cheese infused dips, lures one to enjoy this treat.

The Ingredients:
- *mayonnaise, curry powder, tarragon vinegar, garlic clove, horseradish, onion, fresh vegetables*

The Recipe:
- *Mix in a dipping bowl 1 cup mayonnaise, 1 tsp. curry powder, 1 tsp. tarragon vinegar, 1 clove garlic pushed through a press, 1 tsp. horseradish, 1 tsp. grated onion.*
- *Refrigerate to allow flavors to blend.*
- *Serve with fresh vegetables.*

Pat - vegetable display

MI Dark And Stormy

This drink is Joe's specialty and, if Máire and Ben are to be believed, is the ideal companion to their dinner special, Fish Tacos. Joe included MI for Michigan in the name of this cocktail because one vital ingredient is not widely available outside of Michigan. As a purist on such things, Joe recommends using Vernor's Ginger Ale although it may not be found in other less progressive states. If this presents a problem, either import Vernor's from Michigan or use any non-alcoholic ginger beer, as opposed to a different ginger ale but don't call it a MI Dark and Stormy. Joe also states that the best rum for the drink is

Goslings Dark Rum. As Pat and Jack, Mary and Mike and the Royal Couple, all of whom honeymooned in Bermuda know, this rum has been distilled on the island for at least seven generations. Robert and Pamela have a number of bottles, so they will now know what to do with them. Being an island treat, Joe suggests that MI Dark and Stormy is best enjoyed in the vicinity of a large body of water, Lake Erie perhaps.

The Ingredients:
- *rum, ginger ale, candied ginger, lime*

The Recipe:
- *Muddle (smash) a small lump of candied ginger into the bottom of a tumbler.*
- *Add 2-3 ice cubes.*
- *Pour 2 oz. dark rum (Goslings) and 3 oz. ginger ale (Vernors) over the ice and stir.*
- *Squeeze juice of 1 lime wedge into glass and enjoy.*

GTB Appetizer

We are happy to present this interesting concoction, Goat cheese, Tomato and Basil (GTB) appetizer offered from Cait's collection with helpful hints from her Aunt Sheila.

The Ingredients:
- *fresh goat cheese, bread, butter, cherry tomatoes, garlic, reduced balsamic vinegar (Alessi Traditional Premium Balsamic Reduction), basil, olive oil, salt, pepper*

The Recipe:
- *Toast bread with a bit of butter/oil on both sides, under broiler, until golden.*

- *Cut 10-12 cherry tomatoes (number depends on diner count) in half and toss with a couple cloves of diced garlic and a bit of oil. Season with salt and pepper.*
- *Arrange tomatoes on lined baking sheet and roast in oven preheated to 400° for 20-25 minutes.*
- *Spread goat cheese on toast and top with baked cherry tomatoes and chopped basil. Drizzle with balsamic vinegar.*
- *Enjoy, or return to broiler to heat further and melt the goat cheese.*

Daniel – uncomplicated bar tending

Gorgonzola Crostini

This recipe comes from Daniel, one of the "eldest, sagest and most modest" members of the next generation which he created after a cousin-initiated challenge to produce an appetizer for the Christmas, 2014 gathering. According to this gourmet chef, he "wisely (and permanently)" tied his appetizer offering to gorgonzola cheese. Unlike other recipes, this "crowd pleaser" will live on in our hearts, minds …and/or perhaps stomachs.

The Ingredients:
- *Bartlett pears, cream cheese, Gorgonzola cheese, butter, dry sherry, French bread, pecans, rosemary, honey*

The Recipe:
- *Pre-heat grill to 350°-400° F. (medium high). Grill 3 Bartlett pears cut into ¼ inch thick wedges with grill covered, 1-2 minutes on each side until golden.*
- *Combine ½ of an 8 oz. package of softened cream cheese, 4 oz. crumbled Gorgonzola cheese, ¼ cup softened butter and 2 tbsp. dry sherry.*
- *Slice French bread baguette(s) into 36 slices approximately 1 inch thick.*
- *Spread about ½ tbsp. of cheese mixture on each slice.*
- *Top with grilled pears then sprinkle with ½ cup finely chopped, lightly salted roasted pecans, 2 tbs. chopped fresh rosemary (spread over the entire 36 slices) and drizzle with honey.*

Alexa (Chappellet-Flagler) Brooke, Zachary, Robert -
California family hospitality

Wine

Like Beer, Wine is a basic adult beverage. On McMillen Park Drive the selection was primarily restricted to Gallo Hearty Burgundy which made its appearance when spaghetti or lasagne was served and, of course, for the sauce accompanying steaks. At times there was also Chianti, in its classic basket covered bottle, aging in the broom closet while a Waterford decanter in the living room also displayed a red wine.

Reflecting international trends of recent times, we all seem to have become very sophisticated, with a palate for any number of fine vintages appropriate with the meal served. Coincidently, the family has a connection with one of the finest vineyards in Napa Valley. Nanna had a brother, James, who married and had a daughter named Sybil, Dad's only first cousin on Nanna's side of the family. Sybil lived in California and married Cyril Chappellet who in turn had three children including Donn Chappellet, the base generation's second cousin. In the 1960s, Donn and his wife Molly founded the Chappellet Winery near St. Helena, California in Napa Valley which has become world famous. Robert and Pamela met Donn's children (second cousins once-removed), specifically Lygia, Alexa and Dominic who, in keeping with family tradition, were most hospitable and welcoming.

The Ingredients:

- *wine (red, white or rosé)*

The Recipe:

- *For white or rosé, chill wine to refrigerated temperature and serve cold in a stemmed wine glass.*
- *For red wine, serve at room temperature. After opening allow wine to breathe, or pour through an aerator, into a proper wine glass or hock.*

Adjustments:

While the 'rules' for serving wine might include whites for fish or white meats and reds for red meat, modern thinking is to find wines you enjoy and don't bother with the 'rules.' All wine does taste better when using Waterford Chrystal. (Mom used to insist that she would prefer her Waterford broken in use than just sitting on the shelf.) Temperature does effect taste. The colder the wine, the less distinct the flavors become, which is the reason red wines are seldom chilled. Rosés are an ideal compromise, particularly in warmer weather when a cooler refreshment is appropriate.

The Royal Couple – an inventory from the Chappellet Vineyard

Connollys in the Kitchen: Then and Now, 2016

DINNER

Dinner in the Connolly Family was an important time as we gathered around the table in the family room at 4305 nearly every day of the week. Dad would sit at the head of the table with Mom to his right. Next came Pat and the girls in descending order followed by the boys in ascending order so Robert was next to Dad. On special occasions the dinner might move to the dining room. There were exceptions. For example, on Tuesdays when Dad was travelling to South Bend and on most Saturdays, dinner time was more informal. Dad would serve the meat, using his bone-handled carving set, and Mom would dish out the potatoes and vegetables. The eight of us would be served by seniority with Pat first and then down the line. Dad would become a bit annoyed when the boys would be looking for seconds before he had served Mom and himself... timing was crucial when seeking seconds. Dinner started with grace before and ended with grace after. Barring special circumstances, no one was permitted to leave the table before the final grace, or sometimes well after grace. Although Mom would say years later that she regretted the practice - there were poor starving souls in China - we were required to clean our plate before being dismissed.

161

This became quite a hardship for some of the younger girls who weren't keen on staples such as lima beans. We all remember the misery of that last diner looking forlornly at a plate of beans. Occasionally, a few fell below the rim of the plate, onto the floor or were secreted under the knife, it was possible to ease the burden.

Richard, Sheila, Mary, Jack Pat, Anne, John, Joan, Mom - Christmas, 1983

Mom's Pizza

Enjoying Mom's pizza on Saturday night was a regular cold-weather occurrence, usually in the family room with a fire blazing or in later days, with a sporting match of some description on the television. Television was not a big thing in our family. In fact we didn't even own one until the 1960s, although Dad always rented one when the Yankees were in the World Series. We entertained each other with board games and other similarly ancient diversions. Back to the pizza…Mom, with the able assistance of some of us who enjoyed the process, would start with the dough, mixed in the big yellow bowl, kneaded on the family room table and spread onto aluminum pizza pans for doctoring and cooking. The recipe usually allowed for plenty of extra dough which was then used for bread sticks and English muffins. (see Breakfast)

The Ingredients:
- *yeast, salt, flour, olive oil, butter, green onions, sugar, mushrooms, tomato sauce, tomato paste oregano, basil green pepper, pepperoni, ground beef, mozzarella*

The Recipe:
The Dough
- *Soften 2 cakes of yeast or 2 dry packages in 4 cups of lukewarm water.*
- *Add 2 tbsp. of salt.*
- *Slowly add 6 cups of flour and mix well.*
- *Add an additional 5-6 cups of flour kneading dough on a floured board until it is smooth and elastic.*
- *Place dough in a greased bowl and cover with greased wax paper.*
- *Allow to rise until the dough doubles in size…2-3 hours.*
- *Divide into sections for the pizzas reserving any extra for breadsticks and/or English muffins.*
- *Grease pizza pans and spread dough to edges in a thin, consistent crust.*
- *Allow to sit for 10-15 minutes before brushing with oil and adding sauce and fixings.*

The Sauce

- *Melt 2 tbsp. of olive oil and 2 tbsp. of butter.*
- *Add 4 green onions chopped including greens and 1 tsp. sugar.*
- *Sauté slowly in a frying pan for 2 minutes.*
- *Add 6 large mushrooms thinly sliced.*
- *Sauté slowly and set aside.*
- *Mix 1 large can of tomato sauce, 2 6 oz. cans of tomato paste, 1½ tsp. oregano (mashed), 1 tsp. basil, ¼ tsp. salt, dash of pepper, 1 rounded tsp. sugar and 1 tbsp. olive oil.*
- *Blend together and refrigerate.*

The Fixings

- *Sliced pepperoni, browned ground chuck, green peppers, mushrooms, etc. as ordered.*
- *Spread mozzarella on top.*
- *Bake at 400° for 15-20 minutes.*

Adjustments:

We are advised by those who hold the evidence of these secret recipes that the sauce described above, despite its complexity, made these pizzas special. In today's fast moving world, one might be tempted to make adjustments in the interest of shortcuts but this pizza was particularly memorable. Of course, other fixings, including chicken, pineapple, shrimp, ham, tuna fish, anchovies, etc. etc. are acceptable to suit the diner's taste.

Nikki, Eian, Nick, Sean, Cait, Billy - Thanksgiving

Maui Ham

We are quite confident that Mary dreaded the days when ham was served for dinner because inevitably the meal the following day was Maui Ham or Ham Maui depending on who you ask. Eventually, Mom stopped requiring Mary to eat a bit of ham in the event that, "her taste buds had matured." Everyone else, however, greatly enjoyed this meal, perhaps even more than the original ham. Michael particularly became an expert, ensuring it was passed on to the future generations. As proof, Richard and Molly have picked up the gauntlet so that Caroline will have a favorite recipe as well.

The Ingredients:
- *butter, green peppers, canned mushrooms, ham, pineapple/juice, brown sugar, vinegar, soy sauce, cornstarch, Chinese crispy noodles*

The Recipe:
- *Sauté in large frying pan 3 tbsp. butter, 1 cup chopped green peppers, 1 4½ oz. can of mushrooms-drained, 1½ lb. of cooked*

> *ham-cubed, 1 can of pineapple chunks-drained (but set syrup aside).*

- *Mix pineapple juice and top up with water to make 1 ½ cups liquid.*
- *Add ¼ tsp. salt, ½ cup brown sugar, 1/3 cup vinegar, 2 tbsp. soy sauce, 2 tbsp. cornstarch.*
- *Stir sauce into sautéed ingredients at low heat until the sauce thickens.*
- *Serve over rice or Chinese crispy noodles.*

Adjustments

> *This recipe requires little in the way of adjustments and Michael would be annoyed with any such attempts. We're sure he wouldn't have any problem with the modern version of green peppers, which can be red, yellow or orange, or fresh pineapple and/or mushrooms – chopped.*

Colin, Joe, Emily, Mitch, Nikki - Thanksgiving in Monroe

Meat Loaf

Meat Loaf was an especially enjoyed dinner and some of us even ordered it as our special birthday dinner. A word about that... we were permitted to select the dinner menu to be served on our birthday. The most frequently chosen included lamb chops, steak, pizza and lasagna and occasionally something else would sneak in...Meat Loaf. This is Mom's handwritten recipe. However, she also produced a second recipe, typed on her distinctive and ancient Royal typewriter, that added a barbecue sauce. We will include that as well. One notes that the second recipe called for ground round instead of ground chuck which, perhaps, reflected a more prosperous time.

The Ingredients:
- *ground beef/chuck, bread crumbs, onion, egg, salt, tomato sauce*

The Recipe:

Handwritten:
- *Combine in a bowl: 1½ lbs. ground chuck, 1 cup bread crumbs, 1 finely chopped onion.*
- *Mix in small bowl 1 egg, 1½ tsp salt, 1 can tomato sauce.*
- *Add egg/tomato to meat mixture, form into loaf.*
- *Place on baking pan and bake at 350° F. for 1½ hours.*

Typed:
- *Combine in a bowl: 1½ lbs. ground chuck, 1 cup bread crumbs, 1 finely chopped onion.*

- *Mix in small bowl 1 egg, 1½ tsp salt, 1 can tomato sauce.*
- *Add egg/tomato to meat mixture, form into loaf.*
- *In a mixing bowl combine 2 cans tomato sauce, ½ cup water, 3 tbsp. vinegar, 3 tbsp. brown sugar, 2 tbsp. prepared mustard, 2 tbsp. Worcestershire sauce.*
- *Baste the meatloaf with the marinade.*
- *Place on baking pan and bake at 350° F. for 1½ hours.*

Adjustments:

Apart from using ground round instead of ground chuck, Mom suggested that some people might like to add green peppers. Michael claims there is no better lunch than left-over meat loaf with a bit of ketchup, lettuce and Swiss cheese.

Colin and Cait – carver and adviser

Perfect Rib Roast

The recipe is courtesy of Cal O'Connor. Cooking meat in an oven is always a tricky proposition because one wants a crispy exterior without overcooking the interior. Kevin's Mom swore by this recipe, a favorite in the O'Connor household. Since Joan has passed it on, we assume it is now used by the next generation. According to Mrs. O'Connor the cooking process described in this recipe allows one to begin cooking well in advance of serving and works well with any size roast.

The Ingredients:
- *rib roast, salt, pepper*

The Recipe:
- *Remove roast from fridge to bring to room temperature.*
- *Pre-heat oven to 375° F.*
- *Salt and pepper roast…but add no flour.*
- *Place roast in pre-heated oven for 1 hour and after that time turn the oven off but do not open the door.*
- *45 minutes before serving, turn the oven to 300° F. to warm.*

Adjustments:
We would not dream of suggesting any adjustment to this recipe except, perhaps, to use sea salt instead of ordinary table salt, but then that would be an adjustment for most recipes calling for salt.

Jack – carving the beast

Baked Ham

Ham was frequently served, much to Mary's chagrin. The process was not particularly complicated as it was possible to purchase hams which had been precooked to varying degrees. Honey baked hams were a favorite as they came pre-cut rotationally around the bone and had a crunchy sugary glaze. In Ireland, ham is purchased in a more natural state and Pamela has perfected the art of preparing one - important because it is a staple, with turkey, at Christmas time.

The Ingredients:
- *large bottle of full sugar cola, cloves, glacé cherries, dark brown sugar, Dijon mustard, honey*

The Recipe:
- *Soak ham overnight in water to remove salt.*

170

- *Place ham in large pot, cover with water and bring to a boil.*
- *Pour off water and replace with enough regular cola to cover the entire ham.*
- *Bring cola/ham to the boil, reduce heat and cook for 20 minutes per pound.*
- *Remove from pot and with a sharp knife remove the layer of skin leaving the fat on the ham.*
- *Place two layers of aluminum foil on a baking tin, one lengthwise and one widthwise with enough overlap to cover the ham which is placed in the center.*
- *Score the fat in a diamond pattern using a sharp knife.*
- *Mix honey with Dijon mustard in a ratio of one part honey to five parts mustard with enough mixture to liberally cover the ham.*
- *Spread the honey/mustard evenly over the ham using the back of a soup spoon to ensure it oozes into the diamond scores.*
- *Cut glacé (or maraschino) cherries in half and alternate placing a half cherry or a clove in the diamond shapes.*
- *Sprinkle ham with dark brown sugar.*
- *Bake ham in an oven pre-heated to 450° F. for 30 minutes, then turn off oven and allow to cool in the oven for an additional 30 minutes.*
- *Remove from oven, cover with foil and allow to rest for at least 20 minutes before serving.*

Pamela - and this is what it looks like

Lasagna

Pat was the one who introduced lasagna to family dinners as an alternative to spaghetti with meat sauce, called Spaghetti Bolognaise in other parts of the world. Although it may not have been in her initial arsenal, Mom adopted this excellent lasagna recipe which was always a favorite and occasionally chosen as a special birthday treat.

The Ingredients:
- *Ground beef/round, canned tomatoes, tomato sauce, tomato juice, Tabasco, red*

172

wine, salt, lasagna noodles, mozzarella, parmesan cheese

The Recipe:

- *Brown 2 lbs. ground round steak in a frying pan.*
- *Mix in a bowl 1 can tomatoes, 1 can tomato sauce, 1 can tomato juice, dash of Tabasco, splash of red wine, dash of salt.*
- *Add tomato mixture to ground steak.*
- *Boil lasagna noodles until al dente per the instructions on the package.*
- *Layer in deep baking pan, thin layer of meat sauce, 3 noodles, layer of meat sauce, shake of garlic salt and oregano, layer of cottage cheese, layer of mozzarella, shake of grated parmesan, layer of noodles, layer of meat sauce.*
- *Bake at 350° F. for 45 minutes to an hour.*

Adjustments:

Although the layers described in this recipe are Connolly traditions, they can be varied to suit the chef, including adding more cheese, fresh parmesan, meat or noodle layers. In addition, some lasagna specialists claim that the sauce can be varied adding or deleting ingredients as the spirit moves. Some suggest that leaving the pan in the refrigerator over-night allows the flavors to blend with each other.

Kasey, Eian, Billy, Emily, Sean, Patrick – Thanksgiving in Monroe

Beer Pot Roast

This recipe was given to Joan by her good friend and Xavier roommate, Peggy Delany. Although it is certainly not gluten free, or a particularly healthy option, Joan serves it all winter long to put a bit of meat and subsequently warmth, on her family's bones.

The Ingredients:
- *chuck roast, olive oil beer, dried onion soup ketchup, carrots, potatoes*

The Recipe:
- *Brown chuck roast in pot coated with 3 tbsp. olive oil for 15 – 20 minutes.*
- *Pour over meat, ¾ can of beer, (knock back the remainder), 1 package Lipton onion soup, and ½ cup water.*
- *Thinly cover the top of the meat with ketchup, cover pot and bring to a boil.*
- *Reduce heat to low and simmer for 2 hours until tender.*

- *Add pealed chopped carrots and potatoes cooking for about 45 minutes until tender.*
- *Serve hot with noodles or potatoes.*

Joe, Nikki, Daniel, Kaz, Colin, Máire, Chris, Cait, Billy
Thanksgiving – "nearly grown-up" table

Beef Burgundy

During the cold winter months, Mom would frequently serve pot roast which was similar to the beer pot roast recipe. Rather than repeating the recipe, we have included a variation which was served on a number of occasions. The difficulty with this recipe is that it required previous day preparation and overnight refrigeration, not always possible for a number of reasons, including no room in the fridge. Mary and Anne discovered this recipe while digging.

The Ingredients:
- *stew meat, canned celery soup, canned mushroom soup, burgundy, garlic salt, noodles*

175

The Recipe:

- *Combine in a bowl 2 lbs. cubed stew meat, 1 can cream of celery soup and one can mushroom soup, ¼ cup burgundy, good shake of garlic salt.*
- *Place all ingredients in 9x13 baking dish and refrigerate over night.*
- *Bake at 325° F. for 2-3 hours.*
- *Serve over noodles.*

Adjustments:

Like many of Mom's recipes, ingredients were subject to change depending on what was available. Typically, a large bottle of Gallo Hearty Burgundy was chilling in the fridge waiting to be served with steak or spaghetti or added to recipes requiring a drop of vino. In her recipe, however, Mom calls for "whatever you have handy" which includes cooking sherry. A package of onion soup can replace the garlic salt.

Sean, Máire, Katy, Kaz, Cait, Kasey, Dan, Colin, Billy, Conor – giving thanks

Glazed Creole Shrimp

Joan perfected this recipe when Kevin and herself were living in Houston, Texas. With plenty of fresh gulf shrimp available, it became a delicious go-to meal. When the family moved back to South Bend, the recipe followed. Although the shrimp arrives frozen, it remains a tasty meal.

The Ingredients:
- *onion, garlic, butter celery, green pepper, bay leaf, tomato sauce, catsup, dry white wine, molasses, prepared mustard, Worcestershire sauce, shrimp*

The Recipe:

- *Sauté in a large saucepan 1 cup chopped onion, 1 clove minced garlic, 1 tbsp. butter.*
- *Add ½ cup chopped celery, ½ cup chopped green pepper, ¼-½ tsp. ground red pepper, 1 bay leaf, 1 8 oz. can tomato sauce, ½ cup catsup, 1 tbsp. dry white wine.*
- *Cover saucepan and simmer, 20-25 minutes then remove bay leaf.*
- *Mix in a cooking pot 2 tbsp. butter, 2 tbsp. dry white wine, 2 tbsp. light molasses, 2 tbsp. prepared mustard, 1 tbsp. Worcestershire sauce, bring to boil then reduce heat to medium high.*
- *Add 1 lb. fresh (thawed frozen) shrimp peeled and de-veined.*
- *Cover and cook at medium high for 3-5 minutes.*
- *Pour sauce over cooked shrimp and serve over rice.*

Cait, Sean, Billy, Emily, Liam, Daniel, Patrick, Colin, Katy, John -
Easter in South Bend

Roast Turkey

Without question, Turkey was traditionally reserved for Christmas and Thanksgiving. In recent years, the family has branched into beef tenderloin at Christmas while the Ireland branch of the family, as is the tradition in that country, serves ham with the turkey at Christmas. We all recall discussions about acquiring and cooking the bird; for example, self-basting, butter ball, fresh, frozen, etc. etc. When the day came, however, a turkey was ready to be stuffed and cooked. While the recipe below adds one detail (a brine for marinating) that was never part of the traditional Fort Wayne or Monroe turkey. It is offered because it has met with universal acclaim in Ireland and the United Kingdom for ensuring the meat is moist and tender and making no difference in the cooking.

The Ingredients:
- *turkey, buttermilk, sea salt, pepper oranges, garlic, rosemary, onion, butter parsley*

The Recipe:

36 to 48 hours before cooking
- *Mix in a large bowl 3½ pints (2 liters) buttermilk, 3 tbsp. sea salt, 2 tsp. ground pepper, 2 sliced oranges, 1 garlic bulb-separated and sliced, several fresh rosemary sprigs.*
- *Place thawed turkey (11 pounds) into a large cooking bag and add the buttermilk concoction.*
- *Place bag into refrigerator until time to cook.*

On day of cooking
- *Remove turkey from cooking bag and pour off brine.*
- *Stuff turkey with 2 quartered oranges, 1 onion sliced into chucks, several garlic cloves.*
- *Mix in a small bowl 3 oz. softened butter, 1 crushed garlic clove, 1 orange rind, 1 tsp. chopped parsley, 1 tsp. chopped rosemary.*
- *Massage butter mixture under the skin on the breast side of the turkey.*
- *Cook in baking pan at 325° F. for 20 minutes per pound plus 20 minutes (confirm meat temperature with thermometer before removing) and let rest, covered with foil for 20 minutes before serving.*

Adjustments:
Nearly every chef has their own idea about preparing and cooking the turkey. There are a wide range of opinions about what a turkey should be stuffed with or, whether a turkey should be

179

stuffed at all. Joe cooks the bird upside down for the first part of the process. Others cover the turkey during the first hour or so before removing the foil so the skin crisps, and then cover the skin with bacon, which also crisps protecting the bird from burning. Some wrap the ends of the wings and legs in aluminum foil to prevent burning. Any adjustment can work so experimentation is appropriate. Parenthetically, Pamela and Robert have introduced Thanksgiving Day to Ireland, often cooking a turkey crown prepared with the buttermilk brine.

Sheila, Harumi, Jack, Yuji, Lauren, Julie - thankful.

Beef and Murphy Stew

This traditional recipe comes from Brendan and Aileen Goggin. In most parts of Ireland this stew would be known as Beef and Guinness Stew but as all proper residents of the Rebel County know, Murphy's Stout is far superior to Guinness, at least in

Cork. Since Gram was born in Cork and as a result our family ancestry is deeply rooted in Cork, (not to mention our significant Murphy blood) we have no problem with Beef and Murphy Stew.

The Ingredients:
- beef brisket, vegetable oil, onions, flour, Murphy's Stout, carrots, thyme, bay leaf, garlic, salt, pepper

The Recipe:
- *Chop 3 lbs. of beef brisket into bite sized pieces and brown the meat in 4 tbsp. vegetable oil in a large flameproof casserole.*
- *Remove beef and set aside.*
- *Add 2 good sized onions, peeled and chopped to the casserole and sauté for 10 minutes until they just begin to color.*
- *Lower the heat and return the meat to the casserole.*
- *Add 1 heaped teaspoon of flour and cook, stirring for 2 minutes.*
- *Stir in 1 pint of Murphy's Stout along with 3 carrots, peeled and sliced, 1 sprig of thyme, 1 bay leaf and 1 crushed garlic clove.*
- *Season with a dash of salt and pepper then bring to a simmering point.*
- *Transfer to an oven preheated to 275° F. and cook for 1½ hours until meat is tender.*
- *Serve hot in a bowl or over potatoes.*

Adjustment:
In the unlikely event that Murphy's Stout is not available, it is permissible to use Guinness Stout.

Shepherd's Pie

This is a distinctively Irish recipe coming from across the sea and might be a valuable tool in answering the question…what does one do with leftovers? Mom used to package and freeze leftover mash potatoes which, when enough packages were collected, would reappear, baked with a crispy top. Saving the mash potatoes is the first step in Shepherd's Pie. The recipe listed here included leftover leg of lamb but, alternatives are also available.

The Ingredients:
- *leftover lamb, mint sauce, carrots, onions, rosemary, Worcestershire sauce, butter, oil, paprika*

The Recipe:
- *Cut leftover lamb into bite sized pieces eliminating all fat, bone or grizzle.*
- *In a large frying pan/wok sauté 1 large minced onion, 2 chopped blanched carrots, and the lamb until the mixture is hot.*
- *Add a several dashes of Worcestershire sauce, a good shake of dried rosemary and 2-3 tbsp. mint sauce and mix while continuing to heat. The amount of seasoning depends on the taste of the chef.*
- *Pour re-cooked meat and sauce into a glass baking dish/bowl.*
- *Cover the meat mixture with mash potatoes spreading the mash evenly so that the entire surface is covered.*
- *Sprinkle paprika over the potato and then add several thin slices of butter across the top.*

- *Bake for 20-25 minutes, or until the top is golden, in an oven preheated to 350° F.*
- *Serve hot including potato and meat in each portion.*

Adjustments:
Being a leftover recipe, alternatives are as numerous as the chef's imagination. Just create a thick stew with leftover meat, cover with mash potatoes/butter and bake. Left over beef would probably not include the mint, but perhaps a tomato/barbecue sauce and mushrooms. Even turkey might be used with blanched celery or other vegetables and whatever seasonings seem appropriate...experiment.

Katy, Máire, Chris, Kaz – giving thanks

Beer Can Chicken

This recipe was suggested some years ago by Kevin...why does that not surprise us? The original idea was fairly basic, cut the top off a can of beer, plunk a whole chicken down on the can, and cook on a covered grill. The idea is that beer keeps the chicken moist and by standing the chicken up, it doesn't have to be turned. We all remember Dad, slowly and methodically turning the rack of the grill...or appointed one of us to turn it while he was making cocktails or was otherwise occupied. A gas grill must be on indirect heat; coals stacked to the sides for a Weber grill, lest the dripping chicken fat cause a conflagration. The concept has been civilized in more recent years as several companies, including Weber, have developed a pan with raised prongs, doing the job of the beer can. The idea is that the beer goes into the pan and the chicken is pushed down onto the prongs. This recipe is popular on both sides of the Atlantic as it delivers a perfect, rotisserie-style chicken, every time. Since Pamela and Robert cook this chicken on average of twice a month, we will use their basic recipe which is subject to all measure of adjustments.

The Ingredients:
- *chicken, olive oil thyme, basil (any seasoning), sea salt, pepper, paprika*

The Recipe:
- *Brush a whole chicken (any size) with olive oil infused with thyme, basil, oregano, rosemary, mixed seasoning or whatever looks good on your spice rack.*
- *Grind sea salt and black pepper so that it sticks to the oil.*
- *Shake paprika over the entire chicken*
- *Place on the pronged holder on the Weber grill (medium indirect heat,) and fill the pan with beer and cook for one hour.*
- *Or, place holder in oven at 350 °F. and bake for one hour.*
- *Using meat thermometer check temperature at thickest part of breast to ensure the bird is cooked through.*

Adjustments:

There is no particular reason to use beer as nearly any liquid, including water, will keep the chicken moist - although using some actual beverage, whether it is beer, wine, or even cola or 7Up will add flavor. Some people add spices to the liquid or even a bit of liquid smoke. It is a good idea to confirm the temperature of the chicken with a meat thermometer before removing from the grill/oven to ensure it is well cooked. The beer-can method keeps the meat moist even if it is slightly overcooked.

Robert and Kevin - early days

Robert and Kevin - experts

Paella

Julie has added a whole different range of specialties to the family recipes which are greatly appreciated, by those residing at 1212 Maxine as well as those at pool parties and Christmas dinner. She is not only an excellent chef but has the patience for cooking a specialized recipe like paella. Having tasted the original during a State visit to Spain, the Royal Couple finds this to be an excellent interpretation...especially with a pitcher of Sangria (see Happy Hour.)

The Ingredients:

- olive oil, garlic, chicken, pork, onions rice (paella or saffron) chicken stock, white wine, rice, peas, tomatoes, shrimp, scallops, parmesan cheese, paprika, pimentos, lemon

The Recipe:

- Sauté in a large frying pan, ¼ cup olive oil, 6 minced garlic cloves, 2-3 boneless chicken breasts-cubed, 1-2 lbs. pork-cubed (or 1 package linked sausage) until well cooked and set aside.
- Sauté in a second pan ¼ cup olive oil, 2 large finely chopped onions and 2 cups rice (paella or saffron) until onions are browned.
- Place rice mixture into a 9x13 casserole dish.
- Boil 3 cups chicken stock and add 1 cup white wine then pour mixture over onions/rice.
- Arrange on top of the rice, 2 cups peas, 2 large diced tomatoes, 12 shrimp-shell and tail off, 12 scallops, ¼ cup fresh parmesan cheese and ½ tsp paprika sprinkled on top.
- Bake on bottom shelf of oven at 400° F. for 35-40 minutes.
- Remove from oven and cover with towel and let rest for 5 minutes.
- Sprinkle 1 jar of pimentos and arrange 12 lemon wedges on top.

Adjustments:

Julie prefers to use pre-cooked linked sausages rather than pork. Since they don't require as much cooking, they can be added when the chicken is *nearly done. Some chefs might experiment with different base meats, fish or shellfish depending on what is available and what sounds good. It is always permissible to vary quantities of ingredients, or eliminating something altogether.*

Billy, Cormac, Lauren, Dan, Colin - Thanksgiving

Thyme Chicken

This is another offering from Julie's kitchen although Mom passed the recipe on to her. Chicken has always been a staple in the Connolly family whether grilled outdoors with a bit of wine and butter sauce or Mom's baked crispy version, prepared as part a picnic lunch when on a family road trip including the annual visit to Gram. Mom also experimented with chicken casseroles from time to time when she encountered an interesting recipe. This adaptation has become Julie's chicken specialty, quick and easy to cook.

The Ingredients:
- chicken, flour, seasoned salt, butter, olive oil, thyme, cooking wine

The Recipe:
- *Mix ½ - ¾ cup flour with ¾ tsp. seasoned salt (pink paprika) in a bowl.*
- *Heat in skillet 1 to 1½ tbsp. butter and an equal amount of olive oil.*
- *Coat 4-6 skinless chicken breasts in flour mixture and sauté in skillet until brown on each side.*
- *Sprinkle with 1 tsp. thyme and enough cooking wine (sherry) to almost cover the chicken.*
- *Place lid on skillet and cook for approximately ½ hour.*
- *Serve hot.*

Conor, Molly, Richard, Sean - plenty of wine

Dinner Omelet

While an omelet is generally considered a breakfast treat, Pamela has perfected a dinner omelet which utilizes whatever might be kicking around in the back of the refrigerator/freezer. Pamela and Robert enjoy this alternative meal, particularly after Thanksgiving and Christmas when there are turkey or ham leftovers to be finished. Most of the Connolly clan has inherited or acquired a cast iron frying pan, ideal for cooking steaks and corned beef hash. Robert inherited Gram's iron skillet which, after nearly 100 years, is so smooth that it is virtually non-stick, far better than any Teflon, and ideal for this recipe.

The Ingredients:
- *butter, olive oil, onion, meat (turkey/ham etc.) sea salt, pepper, eggs, cheddar*

The Recipe:
- *Sauté in cast iron frying pan 1 tsp. butter and splash of olive oil 1 large diced onion until softened.*
- *Add meat of choice (turkey, ham etc.) and finely chopped sweet pepper, sprinkling of sea salt and pepper and heat well.*
- *Add 4 large slightly-beaten eggs.*
- *As eggs harden lift edges to allow more egg around the sides which adds thickness to the omelet.*
- *Cook 2 – 3 minutes and then sprinkle 2 cups of grated cheddar on top of omelet.*
- *Move pan to oven and bake at 400° F. until cheese is bubbling.*
- *Serve hot.*

Adjustments:
This meal provides scope for an almost infinite number of adjustments. Any meat or fish is acceptable, as would be mushrooms and other types of cheese. Pamela will often add bacon bits if they are available. A leftover turkey omelet is great with leftover cranberries.

John, Mike, Jack, Anne, Dede - Thanksgiving, Monroe

Fish Tacos

This recipe is courtesy of Máire and Ben. Some of us were introduced to their specialty during a Christmas in Key West, but judging from their expertise, that wasn't the first time it was enjoyed. In the case of Key West, there was plenty of Kingfish (not unlike yellow fin tuna) left over from the previous evening's meal so that provided an ideal base. Apparently any meaty fish will do. It is claimed that Fish Tacos are best served with Joe's "MI Dark and Stormy" (see Happy Hour) and when there are plenty of family to enjoy the feast.

The Ingredients:
- *onions, cilantro, fat-free mayonnaise, sour cream, lime, salt, garlic, cumin, coriander, paprika, red pepper, garlic powder, red snapper filets (fish), cabbage, taco shells/tortilla wraps*

The Recipe:
The Crema
- *Mix in small bowl ¼ cup finely sliced green onions, ¼ cup chopped fresh cilantro, 3 tbsp. fat free mayonnaise, 3 tbsp. reduced fat sour cream, 1 tsp. grated lime rind, 1½ tsp. fresh lime juice, ¼ tsp. salt, 1 minced garlic clove.*
- *Set mixture aside*

The Filling
- *Mix in small bowl 1 tsp. ground cumin, 1 tsp. ground coriander, ½ tsp. smoked paprika, ¼ tsp. ground red pepper, 1/8 tsp. salt, 1/8 tsp. garlic powder.*
- *Sprinkle mixture on both sides of 1½ lbs. red snapper fillets and place fish on greased cooking sheet.*
- *Preheat oven at 425° F. and bake fish for 9 minutes or until fillets flake easily when tested with a fork.*
- *Remove fish to serving bowl and break into pieces.*

The Tacos
- *Warm taco shells or tortillas.*
- *Shred 2 cups cabbage.*
- *Fill taco shell/tortilla with fish, cabbage and top with 1 tbsp. crema.*
- *Enjoy.*

Adjustments:
The most important ingredient in this recipe is fish so it is not necessary to restrict the menu to red snapper. Yellow fin tuna or Kingfish (as was the case in Key West) and any other firm and meaty fish will also work. If the fish has been previously cooked, all that is necessary is to rewarm and add the filling spices.

Ben and Máire – Fish Tacos coming up

Tuna Florentine

This recipe must from ancient archives. According to the recipe card, it comes from the kitchen of Eileen Murphy Connolly. We don't recall too many occasions when Mom was referred to including her maiden name. This is obviously a healthy meal with tuna and spinach but, as it only serves four, she would definitely have trebled the recipe. Once again, Anne and Mary came across this dish in their collections.

The Ingredients:
- *frozen spinach, canned tuna, lemon juice, canned mushroom soup, fried onion*

The Recipe:
- Heat one package frozen spinach in a small amount of water until thawed.
- Drain and place in a shallow 1½ quart baking dish.
- Top with chunks of canned, drained tuna.
- Combine 1 tsp. lemon juice with 1 can mushroom soup.
- Pour soup/lemon over tuna/spinach.
- Bake uncovered at 350° F. for 20 minutes.
- Top with 1 can, fried onion rings and cook an additional 10 minutes.
- Serve hot.

Adjustments:
Substituting chicken or turkey for the tuna on the bed of spinach would also make for a delectable Florentine dish.

Cait, Kyoko, Máire - thank heaven for pretty girls

Sour Cream Chicken

This recipe enters the Connolly domain courtesy of Molly and the Evans family. Since we have the e-mails from Molly's Mom, we can be sure this is the real deal. It has become a bi-weekly favorite at the Indianapolis branch of the family and, as Molly explains, starts with healthy chicken and then gets good.

The Ingredients:
- *chicken, sour cream, lemon juice, garlic salt, pepper, Worcestershire sauce, wheat germ, bread crumbs, margarine, salt, paprika*

The Recipe:
- *Combine in a mixing bowl 1 cup sour cream, 1 tsp. lemon juice, ½ tsp. garlic salt, ¼ tsp. paprika, ½ tsp. salt, ½ tsp. pepper, 2 tsp. Worcestershire sauce.*
- *Roll 8 boneless chicken breasts in sour cream mixture.*
- *Remove breasts one at a time leaving as much mixture on the chicken as possible.*
- *Mix equal portions of bread crumbs and wheat germ.*
- *Roll creamed chicken breasts into bread crumbs/wheat germ and then roll up each breast into a ball shape.*
- *Place rolled breasts into a 9x13 baking dish.*
- *Pour melted margarine over chicken and cover with foil.*
- *Bake at 350° F. for 1 hour.*
- *Remove foil and continue baking for 15 minutes.*

- *Serve with baked potatoes, cranberry sauce and rolls.*

Robert and Michael - the Weber

Mizithra Cheese Pasta

Establishing once again, that Julie is the queen of exotic recipes this is another unfamiliar to some of us. Mr. Google tells us that Mizithra Cheese is originally from Crete but has spread throughout Greece and is made with goat/sheep's milk and whey. Julie advises that this specialty is available at bigger Kroger stores and Murray's Cheese stores and that this pasta is great for feeding a crowd.

The Ingredients:
- *spaghetti, Mizithra cheese, butter, garlic, olive oil*

The Recipe:
- *Cook 1 lb. spaghetti per package instructions and drain.*
- *Place spaghetti in 9x13 baking dish.*
- *Sprinkle with 2-2½ cups grated Mizithra cheese.*
- *Melt in a skillet 1½ sticks of butter and continue to cook until it begins to brown.*
- *Add: 1-1½ tbsp. minced garlic (from jar) and sauté for a few minutes.*
- *Pour melted butter/garlic over spaghetti and cheese and toss until combined.*
- *Bake at 350° F. for 10 minutes.*
- *If dish is a bit dry, sprinkle a bit of olive oil after removing from the oven.*
- *Serve hot.*

Alfredo Pesto Spaghetti

Cormac insisted that this recipe be included as it is a favorite in the St. Louis branch of the family. Unfortunately, he didn't have it on hand but he did arrange for his mother to send it on. Anne reports this recipe was originally discovered in one of Mom's "30 minute meal" magazines. Since basil has been plentiful in Anne's garden, pesto alfredo is an ideal use. Hopefully, Cormac and other members of the next generation, will experiment with these recipes when they are required to do a bit of cooking.

The Ingredients:
- *spaghetti, walnuts (pie nuts), basil, garlic, parmesan, milk*

The Recipe:
- *Cook spaghetti as instructed on the package.*
- *Blend in a small food processor: ½ cup walnuts (or pine nuts) 3 cups fresh basil, 2 – 4 cloves garlic, ½ cup grated parmesan cheese until smooth.*
- *Heat slowly in a heavy pot or double boiler 1 cup milk (or 2%) and add blended mixture stirring frequently.*
- *Add 1 cup grated parmesan to the milk mixture and increase heat to allow a low boil, melting the cheese.*
- *Toss drained spaghetti with parmesan/milk mixture and serve hot.*

Welsh Rarebit

When the base generation was growing up, the laws of the Church prohibited eating meat on Friday. This was intended to provide an opportunity for Catholics to make some sacrifice one day a week. However, the law changed (except for Lent) when it became clear that eating excellent fish, or lobster, for example, was hardly a great sacrifice. In those bygone days, Friday generally meant fish. While some fish dishes, i.e. fish sticks, were well-received, others like salt cod, which for some took well into Saturday to chew, were not. Another standard, and favored option was Welsh Rarebit, particularly in the summer and fall when Dad's tomatoes were plentiful.

The Ingredients:
- cheddar cheese, butter, beer, egg, Worcestershire sauce, salt, paprika, red pepper, curry powder, Colman's dry

mustard, French's mustard, Tabasco, pepper, French bread, tomatoes

The Recipe:

- *Grate or shred 1 lb. aged yellow cheddar into a bowl.*
- *Melt in double boiler 1 tbsp. butter and stir in 1 cup beer.*
- *When beer is warm, stir in grated cheese.*
- *Stir continuously until cheese is melted.*
- *Add 1 slightly beaten egg.*
- *Season rarebit with 1 tsp. Worcestershire sauce, 1 tsp. salt, ½ tsp. paprika, dash of red pepper, ½ tsp. curry powder (or pinch of saffron), ¼ tsp. Coleman's dry mustard.*
- *Serve over toasted French bread topped with a slice of tomato.*
- *This recipe serves 6-8 persons.*

Adjustments:

Typically, Mom would use Old English, a processed cheese, far less expensive then aged cheddar, certainly a consideration when serving ten people. In addition, processed cheese melts more consistently then normal cheddar. It is, of course, permissible to experiment with seasonings to taste.

Oven Roasted Salmon

Salmon is a wonderful and tasty fish, especially when prepared according to this recipe, presented by Ewelina. When cooking any family meal, perhaps one of the most important ingredients never makes the ingredient list, as

Ewelina reminds us, when her recipe requires that the marinade be "rubbed with love."

The Ingredients:
- *salmon fillets, brown sugar, smoked paprika, flaked salt, pepper, thyme, barbecue sauce*

The Recipe:
- *Rub salmon fillets 'with love' using a mixture of brown sugar, smoked paprika, flake salt, black pepper and thyme. (measures to taste)*
- *Place salmon, skin side down on a non-stick baking sheet.*
- *Bake salmon in the oven, preheated to 450° F. for 12-15 minutes or until cooked through.*
- *Remove salmon from oven and brush with barbecue sauce.*
- *Return to oven for a short time until sauce bubbles.*
- *Serve hot.*

Steak On An Iron Skillet

Richard would like the opportunity to introduce Cath's steak specialty to Molly and Caroline in Indianapolis and we are happy to oblige. Richard would not remember, because he wasn't born yet, that Dad and Mom also cooked steak on a skillet. For the birthday girl or boy, it was frequently the meal-of-choice. Mom often served lima beans with this meal (not everyone's favorite) perhaps understanding that we so looked forward to the steak that we would tolerate the beans. One significant difference between steak at home and steak at Cath's was that

Cath served filet mignon while, with ten mouths to feed, Dad cooked bone-in sirloin. The basic cooking process was the same but the after-cooking wine sauce was his special treat. That process is included after the 'advice' section below. It goes without saying…although we will say it anyway… any meat, particularly red meat, should be removed from the refrigerator and brought to room temperature before cooking.

The Ingredients:
- *steak, salt, pepper, red wine, butter*

The Recipe:
- *Remove meat from fridge, sprinkle with salt and pepper and allow to warm to room temperature. (Cath used kosher salt but sea salt is also very nice.) (Dad also rubbed garlic into the bone and across the meat.)*
- *Coat base of iron skillet with salt and heat at full flame. (A small drop of water will sizzle when the temperature is correct.)*
- *Cook steak until brown on one side, flip and repeat process.*
- *Advice: Never turn a steak more than once. Remove the steak before it is completely cooked as it will continue to cook off skillet. For a normal sized filet as little as 30 seconds per side will produce medium rare. As the meat cooks, you can determine the rare-well by pushing on the cooked side with your finger. The stiffer the meat, the more it is cooked.*
- *After removing the steak, turn off gas and pour about ½ cup of water onto skillet. This will result in a massive cloud of steam so stand back.*
- *When the steam subsides, scrape the skillet with a spatula dislodging all of the*

meat bits which remain on the skillet and allow water to dissipate.
- *Turn the gas to low heat and pour 1-1½ cups red wine onto skillet with a good sized lump of butter.*
- *Allow wine sauce to simmer for several minute, cooking off the heavy wine taste.*
- *Pour sauce over sirloin steak.*
- *Provide diners with plenty of hard rolls to soak up excess wine sauce after the steak, cut into thin diagonal slices, has be served.*

Michael – enthusiastic steak chef

Lobster Boil

Rarely served more than once a year, nearly everyone's favorite dinner was lobster. That special occasion was typically in June around Dad's birthday when Cath and Nanna came to celebrate. Cath would order live lobsters and steamer clams from Saltwater Farms in Rockport, Maine. The feast was delivered, express/next day delivery, to great excitement, in a tin container about two feet high and eighteen inches across with the clams at the bottom and the lobster packed in seaweed above. The tin container was itself packed into a wooden barrel that left plenty of room for ice above, below and on the sides. (The wooden barrels made great garage storage for baseball bats, sporting equipment or bits of lumber.) When the time came to cook, the lobsters were removed, to the young one's squeals of fright. The seaweed was discarded and the clams, which would serve as the appetizer, were removed and steamed. The lobsters were returned to the tin container. Holes were punched in the lid and the main course was cooked. When all was in order, the picnic table in the back yard was set, for adults only, and the feast served. Meanwhile, the unwashed masses would clamber for the odd leg and the slightest taste of lobster. The idea of actually eating a cheliped was beyond our wildest dreams. Someone, Mary perhaps, discovered that there was actually a thin vein of meat in the antennae of larger lobsters, so even that got a thorough chewing. Nanna was particularly appalled at our rooting through the boneyard in hope of finding some morsel left behind. As we got older, and live lobster could be purchased locally at a more reasonable price, we finally got our chance to enjoy the treat. A visit to Cath became particularly memorable when dinner included a lobster. Cath was not a fast eater at the best of times, but when lobster was involved, the meal could go on for several hours as everyone slowed down, savored the flavor and enjoyed the conversation.

The Ingredients:
- *live Maine (cold water) lobsters, salt, butter*

The Recipe:
- *Fill a pot large enough to cover the lobsters with water.*
- *Add a good measure of salt and bring to a boil.*

- *Taking each lobster high on its back with a pair of tongs, submerge the lobster, head first into the boiling water.*
- *Depending on the size of the pot, it may be possible to cook two or more at one time.*
- *After submerging the lobster, cover the pot and allow the water to return to the boil. When that occurs, the lobsters will be bright red and cooked.*
- *Remove from the water, drain off any excess water and allow the shell to cool.*
- *Laying the lobsters shell down, cut down the middle from the head, between the legs to the tail.*
- *The red stuff is the roe (eggs) and the green is the liver, both of which are delicacies, depending on one's taste.*
- *Serve on a large plate, with melted butter on the side for dipping.*

Adjustments:

There are two schools of thought on cooking lobster. The first is as described in this recipe which quickly puts the lobster out of its misery. The second is to place the lobster into the pot, pour in a few inches of cold salt water, however not enough to cover them. Then turn on the gas which, according to Cath, allows the lobster to slowly drop off to sleep as the temperature rises. When buying lobsters, the best size is 1¼ to 1½ lbs. Larger lobsters do not cook evenly and you can get over-cooked chelipeds and undercooked tail. In addition very large lobsters (three or more pounds) take many years to mature and if they have survived the traps for that long, it is only right to let them live. Finally, make sure there are plenty of napkins available; roll up your sleeves and dig in. Eating lobster is not for the dainty or faint of heart. Remembering our early days, every morsel is to be enjoyed.

Julie, Pat, Harumi - someone must do the dishes

DESSERTS

No meal would be complete without something for the sweet tooth. Apparently, Mom's father, John Murphy would ask Gram, "What's for dessert?" even before the meal was served. It seems our Uncle John Murphy, Mom's brother, continued the practice. When John Connolly began with the same question, Mom was a bit annoyed but not particularly surprised. As they say in Ireland…"the apple (or nut) doesn't fall far from the tree."

Cowboy Cookies

The only place to start with desserts has to be with the now world famous Cowboy Cookies. While I am unsure as to the origins of this sinful treat, we have made them as all long as anyone can remember. It was wonderful to open your lunch bag at St. Henry's and find a cowboy cookie. Unsurprisingly, the slender among us – Joan and Mary – always seem to have these cookies on hand. Although there are several 'tricks of the trade' e.g. soft but not melted butter, those with high end mixers have eliminated all the difficulties.

The Ingredients:
- *flour, butter, baking soda, baking powder, salt, brown sugar, granulated sugar, eggs, vanilla, rolled oats, chocolate chips*

The Recipe:
- *Sift into large bowl 2 cups flour and mix with 1 tsp baking soda, ½ tsp. baking powder, ½ tsp. salt.*
- *Blend in separate bowl 1 cup butter, 1 cup brown sugar, 1 cup granulated sugar.*
- *Add 2 eggs and beat until light and fluffy.*
- *Add flour mixture and mix well.*
- *Add 2 tsp vanilla, 2 cups rolled oats and 1 12 oz. package semi-sweet chocolate morsels and blend.*
- *Drop by teaspoon onto greased cookie sheet. (Some experts do not grease the sheet as the butter prevents sticking.)*
- *Bake at 350° F. for 10-12 minutes.*

Adjustments:
Remarkably, there are some in the next generation of our family who don't like chocolate chips so some dough can be set aside for naked cookies. Others have experimented with raisins and M&Ms but there is nothing like the originals. Please ensure a minimum of raw dough is consumed or there won't be any cookies.

Erin Singleton (Robert and Pamela's Niece) -
making Cowboy Cookies in England

Pie Crust

Among the more ancient recipes this is, perhaps, the most simple. If there was one thing Grammy was an expert at, it was apple pies. When we were growing up, it was always a thrill to "help" Grammy bake the pies and proudly claim participation when dessert was served.

The Ingredients:
- *flour, salt, lard, butter*

The Recipe:
- *Sift 2 cups flour and 1 tsp. salt into a bowl*
- *Add 2/3 cup white lard... or a bit less, replacing the rest of the measure with butter.*

- *Add 4 tbs. tap water, mix and knead and roll out to an approximate thickness of 1/8 inch.*
- *This recipe will make two crusts or one for the top and one for the bottom.*

Pie Filling

While Gram used to fill her pies with plenty of apple, sugar, cinnamon and butter, we have decided that this pie crust should be filled using a recipe from Howth, County Dublin perfected by May Walsh. As any of us who visited May over the years would attest, her Apple Tart, cooked in the Walsh house near the summit of Howth Hill, was a highlight of the visit. The Walshs had a cozy kitchen in the middle of the house in which they, and visitors from across the ocean, spent a great deal of time, particularly if it was cold and damp. Along one wall was an old fashioned Aga stove which not only kept the kitchen warm but produced wonderful baked goods, roasts and full-Irish breakfasts. May was married to Joe Walsh, Mom's second cousin. Joe's father, Frank and Grammy were first cousins and Pat was privileged to witness the reunion of the two when she travelled to Ireland with Gram in 1970. The current Walsh family includes Joan and her family, whom many of us met in Carlsbad, California in the summer of 2015, Carmel who lives in Howth and Denis who lives with his family in County Meath. That generation is our, Pat through Joan's, third cousins. Carmel has graciously provided this recipe which she undoubtedly employed in assisting May on many occasions.

The Ingredients:
- *apples, sugar, cloves*

The Recipe:
- *Peel and thinly slice approximately 2 lbs. cooking apples (where cooking apples are*

208

not available…apparently in California… Carmel suggested green apples.)

- *Mix with ½ to ¾ cup of sugar and place into filling.*
- *Add 5-6 whole cloves.*
- *Cover with top crust or cut top crust into strips to create a weave pattern.*
- *Bake at 425° for 30-35 minutes until crust is brown and filling bubbles.*

Adjustments:

Although the cloves are May's secret ingredient, some people may prefer a coating which includes cinnamon and/or nutmeg. In addition, depending on the season, May might also mix the apples with blueberries and with mincemeat…all of which, we can attest, is delicious.

May and Carmel Walsh – a bit of a tart

Grasshopper Pie

This delicacy is particularly enjoyed at Christmas time and popular on both sides of the Atlantic. Having said that, Robert's first shot in Ireland went a bit astray. The difficulty was that it didn't look green enough so he added a bit more Crème de Menthe. The problem with that was, because of the increase in alcoholic content, the pie didn't freeze leaving a bit of a soupy mess. As a result, Pamela's Aunt Maeve, nearly 90 at the time, who never drank in her life, marveled at how wonderful the pie tasted. This glitch has now been sorted out so the pies are firm.

The Ingredients:
- *Oreo cookies, butter, condensed milk, whipping cream, crème de menthe, crème de cocoa*

The Recipe:
- *Crumble 12 Oreo cookies in a plastic bag.*
- *Form a pie crust using Oreos in a greased pie tin. A bit of butter might be added to more easily form the crust.*
- *Place the crust in the freezer to harden.*
- *Mix 1 can Eagle Brand condensed milk, ½ pint whipping cream (whipped a bit stiff), 3 tbsp. green Crème de Menthe, 2 tbsp. Crème de Cocoa.*
- *Add **green food coloring** if you don't like the color.*
- *Pour mixture into crust and return to freezer.*
- *Serve frozen.*

Adjustments:

Most adjustments are more in the interest of appearance because any change in the ingredients can adversely affect freezing. Among those used is a sprinkling of Oreo crumbs across the top of the pie. To add a little holiday cheer, try using maraschino cherries to create a stylized Christmas tree with half cherries as the ornaments.

Mom, May, Sheila, Joe, Robert - in Howth, County Dublin

Brownies

Chocolate was, and is, a decadent indulgence among most members of the Connolly family. Legend has it that Joan, in an apparent attempt to stop this trend, decided to withhold chocolate from James, her first born. She was quite annoyed when Michael asked the little fellow whether he had ever tried an M&M. Of course, he had not, where upon Michael introduced him to the chocolate bit and Joan's hard work was undone. It was a special treat when a frozen brownie made from packaged mix, was added to our brown bag school lunch. The recipe below was specifically given to Katy by Aunt Cath. Cath had a particular affinity for chocolate, especially after she married John Berg, an expert candy-maker and chocolatier. The recipe met with rave reviews when Cath presented it to neighbors or at Infant of Prague Church functions in Flossmoor.

The Ingredients:

- *flour, double baking powder, salt, butter, chocolate chips, eggs, sugar, vanilla, pecans*

The Recipe

- *Sift 2/3 cup flour into a large bowl.*
- *Add ½ tsp. double baking powder, ¼ tsp. salt.*
- *Sift combination again.*
- *Melt 1/3 cup butter (5½ tbsp.) 1 12 oz. package Hershey's chocolate chips in double boiler or in pot over another pot of boiling water or in a heavy pan at very low heat.*
- *Beat 2 eggs and add ¾ cup sugar to the eggs.*
- *Slowly add chocolate/butter to egg/sugar and blend.*
- *Add this mixture to sifted flour and mix well.*
- *Add ½ cup pecan chips and 1 tsp. vanilla and mix.*
- *Spread batter on a greased 8"x8"x2" pan.*
- *Sprinkle more chocolate chips on top.*
- *Bake at 350° F. for 30-35 minutes.*

Adjustments:

We would not begin to suggest alterations to this most sinful recipe however Pat advises us that the recipe she acquired from Cath, and has used on many occasions, includes a few variations. Option 1: Only half of the chips (not necessarily Hershey) are melted with the butter and the remainder are sprinkled on top of the batter before baking. Option 2: Half the chips are sprinkled over the top of the brownies about 5 minutes before removing from the oven. Upon removing from the oven spread the softened chips over the top like a frosting. Baker's choice - walnuts, pecans or no nuts at all.

Jack and Pat – Easter bunnies

Eclair Cake

This recipe originates with "Aunt" Ev Kronawitter. The Kronawitters, (Larry and Ev) met Mom and Dad at St. Monica's Church in Whitefish Bay and also lived on North Shoreland Avenue. They remained good friends over the years and Aunt

Ev, Mary's godmother, never forgot a birthday or Christmas. This recipe has now become a family favorite in the McManus household. As is the case with brownies and similar desserts, it is particularly decadent; one reason the McManus family spends so much time running.

The Ingredients:

- *butter, flour, eggs, instant pudding, milk, cool whip, vanilla, semi-sweet chocolate chips, sugar*

The Recipe:

- *Boil 1 cup water with 1 stick (¼ lb.) butter in a cooking pot.*
- *Remove from heat.*
- *Stir in 1 cup flour.*
- *Stir in 4 eggs, one at a time.*
- *Spread dough ¼ inch. thick on parchment paper spread over a 10x14 cookie sheet.*
- *Bake in pre-heated oven at 350° F. for 45 minutes then remove and allow to cool.*
- *Mix in separate bowl 2 pkgs. (3 ¾ g.) instant pudding, 2½ cups milk, 8 oz. Cool Whip and 1 tbsp. vanilla.*
- *Beat with mixer and spread over cooled crust.*
- *Melt ½ cup semi-sweet chocolate chips, 4 tbsp. butter over low heat in a saucepan.*
- *Add 1 cup powdered sugar, 1 tsp. vanilla and 2 tbsp. milk.*
- *Drizzle chocolate sauce over crust/pudding.*
- *Chill for at least 45 minutes before serving.*

John, Sheila, Dad – birthday cake…the perfect dessert

Strawberry Pie

Julie acquired this recipe from her grandmother and it is an all-time favorite, especially in the summer when fresh strawberries are in season.

The Ingredients:
- flour, salt, sugar, milk oil, cornstarch, corn syrup, strawberry gelatin, strawberries

The Recipe:
For the Crust
- Blend in a large bowl 1½ cups flour, 1 tsp. salt, 1½ tsp sugar, 2 tbsp. milk and ½ cup oil and knead until dough-like.
- Push around bottom and sides of pie dish, fluting the edges.

- Bake crust at 450° F. for 15-20 minutes and allow to cool.

<u>For the Glaze</u>
- Mix in a saucepan 3 tbsp. cornstarch, 1 cup sugar and 1 cup cold water stirring until cornstarch and sugar are dissolved.
- Add 2 tsp. clear corn syrup.
- Cook at low temperature, stirring constantly until glaze is thick and clear.
- Remove from heat, then add 2 tbsp. strawberry gelatin and 3 drops of red food color.
- Cool slightly.

<u>For the Pie</u>
- Fill pie crust with sliced strawberries.
- Cover with glaze.
- Refrigerate until the glaze is set, serve and enjoy.

Adjustments:

Julie has suggested several possible adjustments beginning with using 1-2 tbsp. strawberry, raspberry or black raspberry jam instead of the strawberry gelatin and red food color. Most importantly, this recipe can use any fruit or combination of fruits including blueberries and/or peaches. Experiment with whatever is seasonal. Finally, a dollop of whipping cream on top is always a good thing.

Richard, Caroline and Molly – 1st birthday... Where do I start?

Butter Pound Cake

Mom maintained that most of her training in the kitchen came from her mother-in-law, Nanna... at least in terms of proper meals.   Apparently, the reason was that Gram was an outstanding baker and dessert specialist, something for the 'sweet tooth,' but not overly concerned with meat and potatoes. We remember one summer Mom suggested that Gram put the hamburger buns in a brown paper bag, splash a bit of water on the outside and put the bag in the over to warm.   Gram was happy to oblige but she neglected to take the buns out of the plastic bag in which they were packed before putting them in the paper bag and oven....what a mess. Despite this, no one could fault Gram on her baking. Gram believed in butter and her Pound Cake was a delightful confection.   Pat presents this recipe, written in Gram's own hand.

The Ingredients:
- *butter, sugar, eggs, cake flour, baking powder, salt, milk, lemon juice, almond extract, lemon rind*

The Recipe:

- Combine 1 cup butter with 2 cups sugar in a large mixing bowl.
- Add 4 unbeaten egg yolks, one at a time, beating the butter/sugar mix well after adding each egg.
- Sift 3 cups cake flour, 2 tsp. baking powder and ½ tsp. salt into a separate bowl.
- Blend flour mix into butter/sugar/egg alternating between adding flour and adding 1 cup milk.
- Stir in ½ tsp. lemon juice, ½ tsp. almond extract, 1 tsp. lemon rind.
- Beat the egg whites from the 4 eggs until fluffy.
- Fold egg whites in cake mixture.
- Pour mixture into a greased cake pan.
- Bake at 350° F. for about 1 hour or until long toothpick comes out clean.
- Serve with cream or ice cream.

Gram...the most beautiful smile

Pumpkin Pie

Among the popular Thanksgiving Day traditions is Pat's traditional Pumpkin and Pumpkin Chiffon Pie. It would be totally inappropriate to include one without the other because they are both greatly appreciated leaving only crumbs when all is said and done. Michael has been entrusted with the very important job of whipping and dolloping the cream onto one's slice or slices of either of these pies, so one would want to stay on his good side. We are also aware of the fact that the chiffon recipe has travelled across the ocean and is hugely popular among those chosen few who have been graced with a glance at this tradition. Although pumpkins are available in Ireland, particularly at Halloween (which as we all know is an ancient Celtic feast) canned pumpkin mix must be imported from the US and pumpkin pulp as not generally consumed. Pat, being the acknowledged expert, does not use the big old pumpkin that was carved as a jack-o-lantern as it is too watery, rather she acquires smaller pie pumpkins. She halves the pumpkin shell, removes the pulp and seeds and bakes the shells to soften the insides. She then scoops out and purees the meat and freezes it in recipe-appropriate sized portions for future.

Traditional Pumpkin Pie

The Ingredients:
- *flour, salt, butter, pumpkin, sugar, cinnamon, ginger, nutmeg, cloves, eggs, milk, evaporated milk, whipping cream, ultra fine sugar*

The Recipe:
<u>For the Crust</u>
- *Mix in large bowl 1 cup sifted flour, ½ tsp. salt, 1/3 cup lard (part butter), 2 tbsp. cold water.*

- *Blend lard into flour and salt mixture until mixture resembles coarse meal.*
- *Add water. Mix lightly and press into a ball.*
- *Roll out to 1/8" thickness. Place in pie pan, covering bottom and sides. Crimp edges high.*

For the Filling
- *Combine in a mixing bowl 1½ cups, pumpkin, ¾ cup sugar, ½ tsp. salt, 1-1¼ tsp. cinnamon, ½-1 tsp. ginger, ¼-½ tsp. nutmeg, ¼-½ tsp. cloves.*
- *Blend in separate bowl 3 slightly beaten eggs, 1¼ cup milk, ¾ cup evaporated milk.*
- *Fold egg mixture into pumpkin mixture.*

For the Pie
- *Pour mixture into highly crimped pie shell.*
- *Bake at 400° F. for 50 minutes or until knife inserted in the middle comes out clean.*
- *Serve with large dollop of whipped cream.*

Adjustments:
Particularly when the pie is part of a major production, like at Thanksgiving, using a frozen pie crust is acceptable but be sure to re-crimp the edges high. There is nothing wrong with using canned pumpkin. Pat typically measures the spices on the heavy side for a bit more flavor. Michael recommends using heavy whipping cream and whipping to soft points, then add ultra-fine baker's sugar, which will easily dissolve, before whipping to finished thickness. He also recommends putting the bowl and beaters in the freezer prior to whipping time.

Pumpkin Chiffon Pie

The Ingredients:
- *graham crackers, sugar, butter, unflavored gelatin, salt, allspice, cinnamon, ginger, nutmeg, milk, eggs, pumpkin, whipping cream, ultra-fine sugar*

The Recipe:
For the Crust
- *Combine 1¼ cups (8½ crackers) finely crushed graham cracker crumbs, ¼ cup sugar and 6 tbsp. melted butter.*
- *Press firmly into 9" pie pan (heap crumbs into 9" pan and then press to evenly shape crust using an 8" pan.) Alternatively, use the back of a large spoon to compress the crumb mixture.*
- *Bake at 375° F for 6-8 minutes or until edges are browned; cool.*

For the Filling
- *Combine in a saucepan 1 envelope unflavored gelatin, ½ cup sugar, ½ tsp. salt, ½ tsp. cinnamon, ½ tsp. allspice, ¼ tsp. ginger, ¼ tsp. nutmeg.*
- *Stir in ¾ cup milk, 2 slightly beaten egg yolks, 1 cup pumpkin.*
- *Cook over medium heat until mixture boils and gelatin dissolves.*
- *Remove from heat and chill until partially set.*
- *Beat 2 egg whites until soft peaks form.*
- *Gradually add ¼ cup ultra-fine sugar and beat to stiff peaks.*
- *Whip ½ cup whipping cream in separate bowl.*

- *Gently fold together: pumpkin mixture, eggs whites and whipped cream.*

For the Pie
- *Pile folded mixture into graham cracker crust.*
- *Chill until firm.*
- *Serve with generous dollop of whipped cream.*

Adjustments:
Once again, in the interest of time savings when serving large crowds, using ready-made crusts is certainly permitted. If ultra-fine sugar is not available, regular sugar will also work. As explained with the traditional pumpkin recipe, follow Michael's suggestions for the dollops of cream.

Michael, Sarah and Harumi – nibbling at the Pumpkin Chiffon Pie

Carrot Cake

Carrot cake is another offering from Julie's kitchen having been passed on to her by her grandmother. One great thing about a great carrot cake is that it sounds so healthy, after all, surely carrots are a vegetable full of all kinds of nutrients. However, it is a few other ingredients that make this recipe delicious sounding so healthy.

The Ingredients:
- *sugar, oil, eggs, flour, cinnamon, baking powder, baking soda, salt, carrots, raisins, walnuts, cream cheese, butter, milk*

The Recipe:
For the Cake
- *Beat 1½ cup oil and 1 1/3 cup sugar in a large bowl.*
- *Add 4 eggs and mix until well incorporated.*
- *Sift 2 cups flour, 2 tsp. cinnamon, 2 tsp. baking powder, 2 tsp. baking soda, 1 tsp. salt.*
- *Blend together egg/sugar mixture with flour mixture and mix well.*
- *Stir in 3 cups shredded carrots, 1 cup raisins, ½ cup chopped walnuts.*
- *Place mixture in greased cake pan (bundt style works well)*
- *Bake at 350° F. for approximately 50 minutes.*

For the Frosting
- *Blend ½ to ¾ brick of cream cheese, 1 lb. butter and enough milk to create a drizzling consistency.*
- *Drizzle over top and sides of the cake.*

Adjustments:
> *Eliminating the nuts is permitted so that it may be enjoyed by those who have difficulties with nuts. The cream cheese frosting available in the baking aisle of the grocery store is also permitted.*

Billy and Katie - celebrating

Raspberry Almond Shortbread Thumbprints

Julie presents this wonderful treat with the most serious admonishment. Under no circumstances will anyone be allowed to bring these treats to a "cookie bringing" or desert potluck which Julie may possibly attend because this is her "go to" for such functions, and she claims to have no backup…wink, wink. At any rate, in fairness to her demands, we pass on this warning and are confident that it will be honored.

The Ingredients:
- *sugar, butter, almond extract, flour, raspberry jam, powdered sugar*

The Recipe:
<u>For the Cookies</u>
- *Combine in a large mixing bowl 2/3 cup sugar, 1 cup softened butter, ½ tsp. almond extract.*
- *Beat at medium speed for 1-2 minutes until creamy.*
- *Reduce beating speed to low and add 2 cups flour beating for 1-2 minutes until well mixed.*
- *Shape dough into 1" balls and place 2 inches apart on greased cookie sheets.*
- *Make indentation in the middle of each ball using your thumb.*
- *Fill each indentation with about ¼ tsp. raspberry jam.*
- *Bake in preheated oven at 350° F. for 14-18 minutes or until edges are slightly browned.*
- *Remove from oven, let stand for 1 minute, remove from cookie sheet and allow to cool.*

<u>For the Glazing</u>
- *Mix in a small bowl 1 cup powdered sugar, 1½ tsp. almond extract, 2-3 tsp. water. (a tiny bit more may be required but take care as a drop too much and the glazing is soup.)*
- *Drizzle glazing on each cookie.*
- *Recipe makes about 3 dozen thumbprints.*

Baileys Cheese Cake

Baileys Cheese Cake is Pamela's 'go to' desert for dinner parties or other extravaganzas that require special treatment. At one 'small' party for Pamela's fellow teachers when Raheny first opened for business, Pamela and Robert prepared two of these treats as well as two pumpkin chiffon cakes, assuming there would be plenty left over for at least a few days...not a chance. In Ireland, lacking graham crackers, the original crust used digestive biscuits but Pamela has adjusted to use Pat's graham cracker crust as it is soooo nice.

The Ingredients:
- *graham crackers, sugar, butter, light cream cheese, double whipping cream, Baileys Irish cream, brandy*

The Recipe:
<u>For the Crust</u>
- *Crush 1¼ cups (8 ½ crackers) into fine graham cracker crumbs.*
- *Add ¼ cup sugar, 6 tbsp. melted butter and mix in large bowl.*
- *Press firmly into 9" pie pan (heap crumbs into 9" pan and then press to evenly shape crust using an 8" pan.*

<u>For the Filling</u>
- *Beat in a bowl until creamy 3 8 oz. tubs of Philadelphia light cream cheese removed from refrigerator and at room temperature.*
- *Add 1 cup double whipping cream and whisk.*
- *Add Bailey's Irish cream to taste (not too much or it will become soupy) as you continue to whisk and then add a healthy splash of brandy.*

226

- *Pour mixture into crust and refrigerate for at least 2 hours before serving.*
- *Serve with a healthy dollop of whipped cream.*

Kathleen (Murphy-Bass), Michael, Hilda, Sheila, John, Mary, Robert, Joan, Kevin, Sean Hayes - the big hurling match

Meringues

For most of us, our first taste of this delight was in Ballincollig, County Cork at the most hospitable home of Monica, Kitty, Ita and Hilda Murphy. These four lovely ladies were Mom's second cousins - as their mother and Gram were first cousins. Although they were all a number of years older than Mom, they (particularly Hilda) had maintained the connection to our family after their mother died and Mom was very close to all the "girls." When we would visit, we would all sit around their cozy fire having a sherry while the sisters would take turn snoozing leaving the others to carry on the conversation. Ita and Hilda, with their cousin Sean Hayes in tow, made the first of many trips to visit us on the occasion of Pat and Jack's wedding and, as it happened, Gram's funeral. A well-remembered highlight of that trip was probably the first hurling match ever played in Fort

Wayne, with Hilda, decked out in a referee's shirt, doing the honors, as you can see in the picture. As for the recipe, Meringues are quite simple to create and an excellent, elegant light desert which is sure to please, while Pavlova is a slight derivation. Pamela presents this recipe …although being allergic to strawberries that option is for others. It is a desert her mother served using Jello rather than fruit.

The Ingredients:
- *eggs, caster sugar, whipping cream, fruit of choice (e.g. pineapple, strawberries, lemon curd etc.)*

The Recipe:
- *Allow 3 large eggs to achieve room temperature, separate the whites from the yokes, and beat the egg whites until they are stiff.*
- *Add 1 cup castor sugar one teaspoon at a time until the mixture is silky looking.*
- *Dollop the mixture onto a baking paper on a baking sheet in rounded mounds using a tablespoon.*
- *Bake at 275° F. for 45 minutes to one hour until the peaks just begin to brown.*
- *Remove from oven and allow to cool slightly, then remove from baking sheet.*
- *Make a sandwich with two meringues, flat side facing inward using well whipped cream as the filler.*
- *Serve the "sandwiches" standing on their side on whatever fruit you like with a bit more whipped cream for good measure.*

Cait and Nick - celebrating

Pavlova

Pavlova, like Meringues, was a favorite dish among our Irish cousins. This recipe is also courtesy of Pamela. Our relationship with the family in Ireland has been maintained through the years with letters between our great-grandmother and her sister, Gram and her aunt, then Gram and the Murphy girls. When Gram and Pat went to Ireland in 1970 not only did Gram meet her second cousins for the first time, but the next generation, including the Goggins and the Walshs. Hopefully, future generations will continue this tradition of remaining in contact with second, third and even more removed cousins, particularly as technology has made it so much easier to achieve.

The Ingredients:
- *eggs, caster sugar, whipping cream, vinegar, fruit of choice (e.g. pineapple, strawberries, lemon curd etc.)*

The Recipe:

- Allow 3 large eggs to achieve room temperature, separate the whites from the yokes, add ¼ tsp. vinegar and beat the egg whites until they are stiff.
- Add 1 cup castor sugar one teaspoon at a time until the mixture is silky looking.
- Spoon the mixture onto the baking sheet covered in baking paper in a round shape about 6-8 inches in diameter.
- Create a hollow in the middle forming the mixture as if it were a pie crust.
- Bake at 300° F. for one hour or until a slight bit of brown begins to show and remove from the oven.
- Turn oven off and remove the pavlova from the baking sheet placing it on a tray.
- Return the tray to the cooling oven and allow the pavlova to cool with the oven.
- Remove cooled pavlova from the oven and fill the hollowed interior with chopped fruit/lemon curd topped with whipped cream.

Adjustments:

In the event your meringues/pavlova don't meet one's exacting standards for elegance, all is not lost. Crumble the baked, cooled egg whites into chunks and using a medium sized glass tumbler, layer crumbled meringues, fruit (chopped or pureed) and cream repeating process to fill the glass. This adjustment is called an Eton Mess.

Conor, Colin, Cait, Cormac - Happy Birthday

Peanut Butter Chocolate Bars

This is another recipe from Cath and John's kitchen, via Anne. John was an expert at creating a wide range of candy, most of which was chocolate based. His sweet treats had no effect on Cath's waistline, nor on his proper round belly, which, after over eighty years, was hardly likely to expand further. However, the rest of us were required to embark on a cold-turkey campaign after a visit.

The Ingredients:
- *yellow cake mix, smooth peanut butter, butter, eggs, chocolate chips, sweet condensed milk, vanilla, coconut, pecans*

231

The Recipe:

<u>For the Crust</u>

- Mix in a large bowl 1 package yellow cake mix, 1 cup smooth peanut butter, 1 stick melted butter, 2 large eggs.
- Using an electric mixer blend thoroughly at a low speed for 2 minutes scraping sides to ensure everything is mixed and batter thickens.
- Reserve 1½ cups of batter for topping.
- Transfer the remaining batter into a greased baking pan. Using fingers spread the mix evenly, ensuring it reaches all sides and corner. Then set aside.

<u>For the Filling</u>

- Mix in heavy saucepan 1 12 oz. package of chocolate chips, 1 14 oz. can of sweet condensed milk, 2 tbsp. butter.
- Heat over low flame until chips and butter are melted and stir until the ingredients are well combined.
- Add 2 tsp. vanilla.
- Stir in "optionals" like coconut or chopped pecans.
- Pour warm filling over prepared crust and spread evenly.

<u>To Finish</u>

- Crumble remaining crust by hand, over the filling.
- Bake at 325° F. for 20-25 minutes until light brown.
- Cool for 30 minutes before cutting into bars.

Fɾench Whipped Cɾeam Tɾuffles

While it would probably be possible to publish an entire book of candy/sweets/dessert recipes originating in the Flossmoor kitchen, we are forced to pick and choose. This recipe is submitted by Mary who would not be a stranger to a sweet tooth. As you will see, preparing these truffles is a painstaking process but well worth it in the end. According to Cath, who transcribed the recipe, John claimed there are no calories involved but that it is important to watch the waistline, just in case.

The Ingredients:
- *chocolate (dark or milk) whipping cream, salt, rum (or vanilla), flavoring*

The Recipe:
- *Melt in saucepan or double boiler 2½ cups of chocolate (dark or milk depending on preference) and cool it to 98-100° maintain the temperature until it is used in the recipe.*
- *In a mixing bowl, whip ½ pint whipping cream fairly stiff until it holds a low peak.*
- *Removing the beater from the bowl, add the chocolate a little at a time stirring vigorously with a stirring paddle.*
- *When all the chocolate is blended, stir in ¼ tsp. salt and ½ tsp rum (or vanilla) flavoring.*
- *Refrigerate beating bowl until contents set.*
- *Remove bowl and beat until fluffy with a stirring paddle. Beat only enough for the batch to become smooth. Keep the contents cool as they should not get too soft and runny.*
- *To form centers for dipping put part of the batch into a cone made from strong wrapping paper or into a decorating bag with a 3/8 to 1/2 inch diameter round tip.*

- *Squeeze round pieces about the size of a quarter and ¾ inches high onto a baking sheet covered with wax paper.*
- *Refrigerate for 1-3 hours or place in a cool place overnight.*
- *When centers are firm, dip in melted chocolate to finish.*

Fruit Slush

This recipe, which comes via Jack's Mom, Lillian Ready, could be a refreshing dessert served with a cookie, or a side for a special breakfast. Adding fresh fruit, perhaps whatever is in season, *such as - peaches, raspberries, apples, melon, kiwi, or blueberries… is strongly and highly recommended. It may be refrozen, with the fresh additions, and defrosted to the slushy state many times.*

The Ingredients:
- *sugar, orange juice, crushed pineapple, bananas, cherries, melons, berries, peaches*

The Recipe:
- *In a large pot, boil 3 cups water and 1½ cup sugar for 3 minutes and then allow to cool.*
- *Add 12 oz. can orange juice, 12 oz. water, 1 large can mandarin orange, 1 large can crushed pineapple, 6 sliced bananas, cherries.*
- *Freeze.*
- *Partially thaw to serve.*

Adjustments:
As this is a fruit desert or a refreshing addition to a special breakfast, fresh fruit, perhaps whatever

is in season, such as peaches, raspberries, apples, melon, kiwi, or blueberries.

Irish Coffee

We will conclude our recipe presentations with an appropriate finish to a fine meal...Irish Coffee. Dr. Ed O'Connor, Dad's great friend and one of few fellow Irishmen in Fort Wayne, introduced this recipe which has been assiduously followed by Robert and several other family members.

The Ingredients:
- *coffee, Irish whiskey, light brown sugar, heavy cream*

The Recipe:
- *Brew coffee (instant is not acceptable).*
- *Mix in a proper Irish coffee glass one heaping teaspoon of light brown sugar and 1½ oz. Irish whiskey, ensuring that the sugar is fully dissolved.*
- *Pour coffee over the whiskey mix to about ½ inch from the top of the glass and mix well.*
- *Using the back of a spoon pour heavy cream over the top of the coffee so that it floats on top.*
- *Do not stir, rather drink the coffee and whiskey through the cool cream.*

Adjustments:
Some people prefer to lightly whip the cream which makes 'floating' it on the coffee that bit easier. In a pinch, regular or granulated sugar,

fully dissolved, is acceptable (although not recommended). Finally, serving Irish coffee late in the evening has a tendency to create 'wide-awake' inebriated persons, so a good brand of decaffeinated coffee is permitted.

Dad and Mom

POST SCRIPT

We are delighted that nearly every member of the family participated in compiling this book. It certainly reflects the strength of our family as well as the extraordinarily good fortune and blessings God has bestowed upon us.

When the "base generation" was growing up, Mom always stressed the importance of family, not only brothers and sisters but aunts, uncles, cousins, in-laws and our more extended family. Perhaps because Mom had no first cousins, it was important to her that her children and her brothers' children not just know each other, but be friends. Every summer, during our trip to Grammy's house, we used to get together with the Chicago Murphys, usually at their home in Country Club Hills. Whenever Uncle Pat, a Navy Officer, was transferred, it usually entailed a cross-country move for the California Murphys, resulting in a major reunion. (Gram eventually had twenty-two grandchildren.) We all cherished those gatherings, even when it meant about a dozen boys camping out together in a backyard tent at 4305 and the uncles and Dad giving assembly line baths to all – in the same bathwater.

In more recent years, we have continued the tradition of getting together whenever possible. Whether it be at an 'official' reunion, as in Milwaukee or Carlsbad, at an ordination, wedding or funeral, reconnecting and reliving past experiences creates wonderful new memories, introduces 'new' cousins and further strengthens our family.

We can only hope that the next generation continues to value the importance of maintaining close family ties, which our Mom so securely instilled in us. We are delighted that whether it be Easter, Christmas, Thanksgiving or some other event, so many of us make the sincere effort to participate. That is what creates future memories and makes our family bond so special.

INDEX

Breakfast and Brunch, 11

Lunch and Soups, 25

Reuben Sandwich, 26
Smokey Gouda Macaroni and Cheese with Bacon, 51
Spiced Lentil Soup with Coconut Milk, 38
Spicy Roasted Vegetable Mac and Cheese, 50
Texas White Chili, 29
Turkey Chili, 31

Sides and Salads, 55

Apple Cashew Salad, 75
Broccoli Salad, 71
Brussels Sprouts, 67
Canarian Potatoes, 74
Candied Sweet Potatoes/Yams, 66
Casa Style Salad, 76
Chinese Chicken Salad, 57
Coleslaw, 70
Deviled Eggs, 82
Far East Celery, 80
Fried Rice, 68
Hard Boiled Eggs, 81
Hawaii Salad, 78
Oven Roasted Asparagus, 79
Potato Casserole, 59
Taco Salad, 58
Turkey Stuffing, 63
Twice Baked Potatoes, 55
Scandinavian Cucumbers, 60
Stuffed Mushrooms, 62
Summer Pasta Salad, 72
Winter Potatoes, 77

Bread and Buns, 85

Beer Bread, 101
Bread Sticks, 94
Crusty French Bread, 102

English Muffins, 94
Irish Brown Bread, 96
Irish Current Bread, 98
Irish Soda Bread, 87
Old Fashioned Brown Bread, 92
Old Fashioned White Bread, 91
Porridge Brown Bread, 93
Scones, 88
Sweet Potato Muffins, 100
Tea, 90
White Potato Bread, 104
Zucchini Bread, 95

Condiments, 107

Chocolate Sauce, 109
Chocolate-Chocolate, 110
Cocktail Sauce, 108
Cranberries (Mom/Michael), 112
Cranberries (Robert/Pamela), 113
Cranberry Sauce, 111
Mint Sauce, 107
Tomato Relish, 114

Happy Hour, 115

Anchovy Spread, 118
Apple Dip, 132
Artichoke Dip, 124
Beer, 122
Cheese Ball, 151
Clam Dip, 121
Crab Spread, 145
Curry Dip, 152
Dandelion Wine, 149
Gorgonzola Crostini, 156
GTB Appetizer, 154

Dinner, 161

Mom's Pizza, 162
Oven Roasted Salmon, 198
Paella, 185
Perfect Rib Roast, 169
Roast Turkey, 178
Shepherd's Pie, 182
Sour Cream Chicken, 194
Steak on an Iron Skillet, 199
Thyme Chicken, 187
Tuna Florentine, 192
Welsh Rarebit, 197

Desserts, 205

Baileys Cheese Cake, 226
Brownies, 211
Butter Pound Cake, 217
Carrot Cake, 223
Cowboy Cookies, 205
Éclair Cake, 213
French Whipped Cream Truffles, 233
Fruit Slush, 234
Grasshopper Pie, 210
Irish Coffee, 235
Meringues, 227
Pavlova, 229
Peanut Butter Chocolate Bars, 231
Pie Crust (Gram's), 207
Pie Filling, 208
Pumpkin Chiffon Pie, 221
Raspberry Almond Shortbread Thumbprints, 224
Strawberry Pie, 215
Traditional Pumpkin Pie, 219

Connollys in the Kitchen: Then and Now, 2016

NOTES

Connollys in the Kitchen: Then and Now, 2016

Connollys in the Kitchen: Then and Now, 2016

Connollys in the Kitchen: Then and Now, 2016